THE LOST WORLD
OF LANGDALE
& OTHER STORIES

By the author

Poetry
Night Bus to Monte Carlo
Thunder Alley
The Visitor's Book
Coleridge Street
Portrait in Black
Used Rhymes

Prose
A Guide to Historic Haworth & the Brontës

THE LOST WORLD
OF LANGDALE
& OTHER STORIES

MARK WARD

.

First published
January 2023

© Mark Ward

The author asserts his moral right to be identified as the author of the work.

All rights reserved. No part of this publication may be reproduced, stored in a retrieval system or transmitted in any form or by any means, electronic, mechanical, photocopying, recording or otherwise, without the prior permission of the publishers

ISBN 978-1-913144-43-2

All photographs Mark Ward (unless otherwise stated)

Cover design
Michael Webster

Author photograph
Annalie Talent

PENNILESS PRESS PUBLICATIONS
Website : www.pennilesspress.co.uk/books

For Tanya and Tim

CONTENTS

Foreword	7
1 Growing Weed on Lord Clitheroe's Estate	9
2 The Lost World of Langdale	11
3 The Longest Tea Break	14
4 Dorothy and the President	16
5 Making Black Pudding	18
6 Cairistiona's Rock and Wildlife on Ulva	20
7 Trespassing on the Duke of Westminster's Land	23
8 Golden Wonder Winds the Church Clock and puts up the Flag	26
9 In Search of the Golden Eagle with Mountain Man	28
10 The only thing missing were the Grizzlies	30
11 A Right Royal Bird	33
12 Bachelors Buttons and Alfred's Cakes	35
13 Man is Born Free and Everywhere He is in Chains	37
14 A Long Way from Kingston	39
15 Dem Bones, Dem Bones	42
16 The Cloths of Gold	45
17 Statistically Speaking	47
18 Divisions	50
19 Blackburn Blues	53
20 The Beggar's Banquet	55
21 High Tides and Shifting Sands	59
22 A Sorry End	62
23 The Italian Job	65
24 A Brief History of the Alehouse	67
25 Now You See It	70
26 Weights and Measures	72
27 When the lake drops, Neptune rises	77
28 Wrecks	80
29 A Subterranean World	82

30 Even the Cows Love it	85
31 Of Sorcery	87
32 The Problem with Africa	90
33 Taking it for Granted	94
34 Austerity Chicken with Colin Marshall	97
35 Michael and the Great Feast	99
36 Seeking out the Thin Places	102
37 Paradise Lane	105
Recipes	109

Foreword

I began writing these blogs in 2013 and continued with it sporadically over the next six years, during which time I relocated from Grasmere to Blackburn. It's been a period of great political and social upheaval, but I wanted to focus on the human aspect. The individuals; their lives, stories, favourite places and culinary skills. It was celebratory; a paean to England, its history, the land and the people. I've always found people who don't make the news to be just as interesting, and often more so, than people who do. It proved to be the case as they invited me into their lives and homes, told me stories and took me to fascinating, and often overlooked places on the doorstep. It was the most rewarding project I've ever undertaken.

The later blogs, seven in total, are social commentaries, focusing on the collective rather than the individual. These I've divided throughout the book for balance and perspective. If history teaches us anything it's that we're stronger together: strength lies in unity, not division. Compassion is also a strength.

I would also like to take this opportunity to thank Michael Webster who worked with me on designing and uploading the weekly content onto the website, along with the cover for this book.

Mark Ward

My Backyard blog 2013 - 2019
www.markwardpoet.co.uk/backyard/

Growing Weed on Lord Clitheroe's Estate

For those checking in for tips on outdoor marijuana cultivation, I'm sorry to disappoint. The weed in question here is Himalayan balsam: introduced into parks and gardens by Victorians with a penchant for the exotic, only to rapidly spread along the country's arteries; the railways, canals, rivers and roads choking the embankments the length and breadth of the country. Around here each summer the river banks are garlanded in their pink flowers. They are non-native, invasive and extremely resilient, with all attempts to eradicate them having had little or no effect and like the rhododendrons are here to stay.

Which got me thinking about what constitutes a native and how long does it take to belong?

It's a valid question with Brexit upon us and people who have lived and worked here for many years being made to feel as if they don't really belong. Likewise, the Windrush scandal had the Home Office deporting people back to Britain's former colony of Jamaica despite having lived here for fifty years. Their residence deemed temporary, while the South Asian community in British Uganda held British passports and were allowed to settle permanently. It seems arbitrary to say the least.

When it comes to flora and fauna the definition is quite specific, with the cut off point for native species being the erosion of the land bridge, separating us from continental Europe at the end of the last Ice Age. Alder and badgers are in, sycamore and brown hares, out – along with ourselves. We, the English/British are not the descendants of those ice age hunter-gatherers, left behind when the seas rose. We are the descendants of migrants from northern and southern Europe who came here and settled in the intervening years. The term Anglo-Saxon was loosely coined to describe the indigenous population after the Norman Conquest. Celts, Saxons, Jutes, Angles, Vikings, descendants of Roman auxiliary troops from Spain, Croatia, Romania. Groups that had over time formed a nation and a common language.

In the last millennium, communities of Flemish, Jewish, German, Irish, French, Italian, African, Caribbean, Polish and near and far eastern people have settled here. It's part of a continuity that's been going on for thousands of years. It doesn't dilute our culture, it is our culture. Which brings me back to what constitutes a native and who is native?

The answer in the scientific sense is none of us. The brown hare, introduced by the Romans 1800 years ago is classed as non-native, which rules out most of us. Referring to ourselves as native or non-native is pointless, where's the cut-off point? National identity is more about a sense of belonging, of kinship and shared cultural and social values. This applies whether your family roots here go back a generation or a millennium.

The Lost World of Langdale

He said he'd show me dinosaurs, but with visibility down to just a few feet, there could've been brontosaurus having a garden party and we wouldn't have known anything about it...

Leo Walmsley lives at the Old Dungeon Ghyll: a climbers' bar and hotel in Great Langdale. He works for the National Trust repairing and building footpaths and his day can begin with a two-mile trek up a mountain to get to work. He's also a free climber who is occasionally called in by local farmers to rescue sheep that have become crag fast on the ledges. He's a great guy with a boyish enthusiasm, who finds a wonder and beauty in the world around him, and the other week he offered me a rare glimpse into the Lost World of Langdale.

It reminded me of when we were kids; finding secret places we thought no one had been to before. We believed, as intrepid explorers, we'd discovered areas new to science and we'd hollow out a den or perch in the low branches of a tree keeping guard. Obviously these days I'm no longer so naïve, but I experienced the same sense of excitement and anticipation when we set out on our adventure.

The slopes of Lingmoor are densely covered in juniper bushes that act as cover for a large variety of insects, plants and mammals that live beneath its canopy. Concealed from birds of prey and inaccessible even to the mountain sheep, it's a haven and a sanctuary for those that have made it their home. We walked along the edge of the tree line until we found an opening then crawled in and began to make our way towards the summit through tangled trees and gnarled twisted roots that were covered in moss and bright green ferns. The guidebooks tell people to avoid this area: there are no paths and no points of reference to take a bearing from. Its nature is such that however many times you venture in you will never take the same route twice. Occasionally we came upon small clearings where exquisite plants and flowers blushed in the dappled sunlight. Leo reckoned that if you took out all the creatures that lived here and suspended them in the air, they would block out the sky. His gentle wisdom and observation are always endearing. 'Never hang your washing on a half moon.' He'd come out with this little gem in the pub a few days earlier: crawling through the thicket, lost and blind, knowing only that we were ascending, I was trying to figure a way of attaching my washing line to the moon without it slipping off – I was getting delirious… He later explained that a half moon brings moisture to the night air so if you put your washing out late it won't dry.

Three hours after setting out we reached the summit. Scratched and bleeding slightly we sat on a rock among heather and cotton grass smoking cigarettes while three buzzards performed a spectacular aerial display across the valley. Leo's lost world is a world in miniature where some of the more fragile species can survive unmolested. The things we'd seen and the path that reveals itself and yet leaves no trace of itself once passed; could never be found again.

The Longest Tea Break

Seathwaite Tuff is a silica rich white volcanic rock that formed in a crater lake over a hundred million years ago. It appears as a two metre wide seam fifteen hundred feet above ground level in the Langdale and Borrowdale ranges in south Cumbria.
It has similar qualities to flint and can be worked, using a harder material, to produce a razor sharp edge; yet its high silica content makes it far more durable and less prone to splitting and accidental breakage. For three thousand years it was used to manufacture axes that were exported throughout Europe. Such was their value they became status symbols: a form of currency, with highly polished versions often placed in the burial mounds of warriors and chiefs. At the dawn of agriculture these axes cleared the forests and changed the landscape of Britain forever.

I know all this because I've just spent a pleasant couple of hours in the company of writer / photographer Bill Birkett; the second in three generations of legendary Cumbrian climbers who between them have opened up well over a hundred new routes graded in difficulty up to as high as E9. Bill was the photographer on many of their expeditions and his images have been widely published in magazines and climbing journals throughout the world.

I'd come to talk about his first visit to the Langdale Axe Factory over thirty years ago. Sketched by Wainwright in the 1930s, its location on the steep scree strewn slopes beneath the Pike of Stickle is only accessible to experienced climbers. On a winter's day he and some fellow enthusiasts went along to explore it for themselves.

The factory is a shallow cave alongside quarry holes and chipping points. Lichen doesn't form on the tuff and the bright white scree on the approach contrasted sharply with the surrounding rock, as though only recently quarried. Evidence of industry was all around them. In one section they came upon a large round granite block, a hammer stone, surrounded by flakes of graded chippings: beside it on a small shelf in a recess were two palm sized boulders of white Scottish granite; smaller hammer stones that were used to shape the axes. The whole scene was so orderly, so perfectly natural it was as though the workmen had simply put down their tools and gone for a tea break.

The axes discovered there have long disappeared: some were taken as souvenirs, others were handed over to museums and a number of them ended up as gap-fillers in the area's dry stone walls.

I'd asked Bill what made the axes so unique. He placed one in my hands. About eight inches long its main body was lozenge shaped; tapered and honed into a flat sharp edge. It was surprisingly light with its rough surface possessing a soft almost silken feel: the silica having the effect of giving it a plastic coating.

Listening to Bill's stories while holding an axe made locally over three thousand years ago from a substance produced when the world we know was still forming, was really quite something.

Dorothy and the President

Pamela Woof is a scholar and author, President of the Wordsworth Trust and widow of Dr Robert Woof whose energy and vision helped create one of the world's great literary museums here in Grasmere. She's also one of the brightest people I know; and this year she, along with curator Jeff Cowton, has put together, using manuscripts and letters, a major exhibition of the life and work of Dorothy Wordsworth.

The Romantic Movement was a social and cultural revolution of the late eighteenth/early nineteenth centuries that challenged and swept aside pre-conceived notions of class and hierarchy and shook the establishment to its core, laying the foundations for our modern society. Exponents grew their hair long, called for equality and social justice and expressed their 'radical' views through politics, art, literature and science. Regarded as dangerous and viewed with suspicion the passage below from the diary of a local parson at the time of the Wordsworth and Coleridges' residence in Somerset gives an insight as to how they were generally perceived.

From the diaries of William Holland, a Somerset parson

Wednesday October 23rd 1799

Went with my wife to Stowey…saw that Democratic hoyden Mrs Coleridge who looked so like a friskey girl or something worse that I was not surprised that a Democratic Libertine should choose her for a wife. The husband gone to London suddenly, no one here can tell why. Met the patron of democrats, Mr Thos Poole who smiled and chatted a little. He was on his grey mare. Satan himself cannot be more false and hypocritical.

Throughout her life Dorothy was regarded as a peripheral figure in the Romantic Movement and her influence on her brother's work was for many years overlooked. His constant companion and confidante, she was with Wordsworth and Coleridge during the conception and production of *Lyrical Ballads*, a book generally regarded as the Romantic Movement's seminal work. Her hand is everywhere: from the sharing of ideas, the copying and re-copying of drafts to the characters and descriptions that find their way from the pages of her journals into her brother's poems.

There is a timeless and effortless style to her writing that makes her so interesting and readable and a major exhibition of her life and work is long overdue.

Pamela is the acclaimed editor of Dorothy's journals, and there are parallels. The exhibition opens a fascinating portal into the minds of two remarkable women.

Making Black Pudding

Donald Woodburn is a local builder who built the Wordsworth Museum here in Grasmere and completed major restoration work on Dove Cottage in the 70s. My job of maintaining Dove Cottage and the grounds has required me to consult with him regularly over the years and his help and advice have been invaluable. Many of our consultations have taken place at Tweedies Bar, the local pub, and on one such occasion he told me this story.

Donald was born in a farmhouse a few miles from Grasmere at a place called Wray, which was then part of northern Lancashire. They had no electricity or refrigeration and they reared pigs and grew potatoes to supplement their larder. He was only a boy at the time but he remembers vividly the process of extracting the pig's blood and preparing the animal for curing.

Once the pig had been selected it was taken to a cellar where the flagged floors had been scrubbed and covered in salt. It was then placed in a sheep crush where its throat was washed and carefully shaved. A warm metal bucket containing a few inches of hot water was placed beneath and a steel rod was then inserted into its throat releasing the blood, which was slowly stirred with a wooden stick until the bucket was full and the poor animal weakened and collapsed in the steel frame. The bucket was then taken to the kitchen and emptied into a pot where it was boiled with oats before being left to cool and solidify. The conditions had to be just right in order for the process to work. The temperature of the room and the blood had to be the same and menstruating women weren't allowed near as it was felt they'd turn the blood 'bad.' The carcass would be shaved and butchered and a mixture of salt and saltpeter was moulded around the joints to prevent them becoming flyblown. They were then hung on hooks and left to cure.

Donald tells of how cruel it was and he still sees those pigs slowly dying before him as the life drained out of them, but it was nearly seventy years ago: they were subsistence farmers and as he says 'that's just what people did back then.'

Blood
by Annalie Talent

When they killed the pig –
slit its throat to make their pudding –
they wouldn't let me come near:
said it was the wrong time;
that I was unclean.

So I crept round the back
of the sty; watched
as they bled it to death.
Who would have thought the old man
to have had so much blood in him?

They brought it to the kitchen in a bucket.
Mother set to work stirring in the oatmeal.
I watched it thicken; thought of the dark stuff
inside me, working its way out in painful clots.

When it was ready to eat,
they tucked in.
I couldn't look:
didn't have the stomach for it.

Cairistiona's Rock and Wild Life on Ulva

Annalie Talent studied literature, writes poetry and works on the education programmes at the Ashmolean and Jane Austen's house at Chawton. Her interests are eighteenth/early nineteenth century paintings and ceramics and photographing wildlife (mainly sheep). We've holidayed together many times and some time ago took a short boat journey from Mull to the Isle of Ulva on Scotland's west coast to go on one of the islands celebrated wildlife walks.

In the early nineteenth century the island's population numbered around eight hundred and its notable visitors included Boswell and Johnson, Walter Scott, the Wordsworths and John Keats, but over the last two hundred years 'clearances' and economic difficulties have reduced the population to just sixteen, making it a haven for sea eagles and other large raptors. But I couldn't get past Cairistiona's Rock.

Cairistiona came from a family of kelp harvesters and was the eldest of three girls. One day a hunk of cheese went missing from the family larder: she accused her younger sibling of the theft and after tying a plaid around her neck, dangled her from the cliff to extract a confession; but the plaid slipped and she fell to her death. Horrified by what she'd done and filled with remorse she went back to the village and told them what had happened. The elders convened, accused her of murder and condemned her to death. She was bound and sewn into a sack then taken out and placed on a rock at low water. The villagers looked on as she was left to drown on the incoming tide.

Lord Byron witnessed a similar incident in Athens when he came across a procession returning from the harbour with a drowned girl in a sack; slung from a pole and being carried by two men at the head of the group. She was a young Muslim girl who'd been accused of infidelity, which he later alluded to in his poem *The Giaour*.

From The Giaour
By Lord Byron
No – reft of all, yet undismayed
But for the thought of Leila slain,
Give me the pleasure with the pain,
So would I live and love again.
I grieve, but not, my holy guide!
For him who dies, but her who died:
She sleeps beneath the wandering wave
Ah! had she but an earthly grave,
This breaking heart and throbbing head
Should seek and share her narrow bed.
She was a form of life and light,
That, seen, became a part of sight;
And rose, where'er I turned mine eye,
The morning-star of memory!

Ulva is a beautiful island and we spent a good half-day walking the coastal paths along the basalt cliffs, but try as I might I couldn't shake the image of Cairistìona from my mind. I kept seeing her, abandoned on the rock watching the tide and silent villagers through the hessian sack.

As for the wildlife: I can record seeing three slugs, two cabbage whites, a common gull and two ticks – discovered later…

Trespassing on the Duke of Westminster's Land

It's difficult to avoid. The aristocracy still owns a third of Britain, with the Duke holding 140,000 acres, including a sizable chunk of Lancashire. It means that any self-respecting boy with a sense of adventure would find it difficult to venture out into the countryside without stepping on an aristocrat's land; and my youth was spent looking out for, or being chased by gamekeepers and wardens for the crime of walking across fields, or in particular, fishing and canoeing in the rivers on my doorstep.

This continued into adulthood and I remember one particular occasion around thirty years ago, when having paddled upriver in my canoe I paused for a break in a pool of still water near the bank.

Get off my land!!!

I looked up to see an irate man, who I assumed to be a gamekeeper, standing on the embankment a few metres away.

I'd had this all my life and responded sarcastically.

"I'm not on the land."

The riverbed and the bank are private property. You have no right to be here.

He concluded with, *I shall be reporting you to the police.*

"Do what you want," I told him, "I'm not on the bed or the embankment – I'm on the water. "

He repeated that it was private property.

I continued exasperated.

"Hang on a minute. Are you trying to tell me that this water, that's fallen as rain in the Pennines and is on its way out to sea, is also yours?"

He pretty much implied it was.

I told him he was being ridiculous and leaving him seething on the bank turned and set off downstream, half expecting to find a policeman waiting for me when I landed.

Here's the rub – unlike most property owners, a hereditary Duke or Lord literally does own everything above, below and passing through his land: a throwback to the Norman feudal system. To put it in perspective, my house in Blackburn is freehold, meaning that I own the land on which the house was built. But that ownership only applies to the surface area. Were a rich mineral seam to be discovered in my backyard I wouldn't be allowed to keep it. The same rule doesn't apply to our hereditary aristocrats, who for centuries have exploited the coal, lead, iron and copper seams on their estates to the benefit of themselves and their descendants.

The former Lord Grosvenor, Duke of Westminster, when asked what advice he could give to young entrepreneurs hoping to get along in life, replied, "Have an ancestor who was a close friend of William the Conqueror." He wasn't joking.

The Norman Conquest began in 1066 and continued over a period of twenty years. It involved the brutal subjugation of the native population whose lands were forfeit and the spoils divided between William and his mercenaries. Former owners became serfs to their new Norman masters as noted in the Domesday Book or Survey. Made to look like consensual transactions, the survey records the transfer of land and property from the legitimate Anglo-Saxon owners to their Norman overlords.

In the Middle Ages this kind of behaviour wasn't unusual. What's remarkable is that a thousand years on the descendants of those mercenaries, amounting to a handful of families, still own the land, continue to exploit it and are still restricting access; in effect hemming the majority population into congested pockets. These considerable estates are still privately owned, despite the majority of the monarch's own formerly extensive land holdings and property, having been transferred to state ownership.

The poet William Blake and notably Thomas Paine tried to readdress the balance, with Paine arguing for the disinherited populace to be compensated for their loss of land and opportunity. Needless to say, Paine was forced into exile and tried for treason in absentia. The issue doesn't get debated in Parliament and to this day a tiny percentage of the male population continue to inherit vast tracts of land by virtue of their birthright. It's telling that there has only ever been one Domesday Survey…

In recent times, various open countryside campaigns have pressured larger landowners into allowing for limited public access in the form of footpaths and picnic areas within their estates. Some, having realised there's more money to be had with two legged creatures roaming the grounds than four legged ones, have embraced it wholeheartedly, with entrance fees and pay-and-display machines. Handing over your hard-earned cash to wander round your own countryside, now that's quite something.

As a child, the Ribble Valley and the Forest of Bowland were in effect my back garden – a place away from the town where we could breathe and be free, albeit never truly liberated. The wardens and gamekeepers saw to that.

This is the ground we walk on, the spaces we inhabit; and while I'm not advocating stripping the young Duke, or anyone else for that matter, of their lands and titles, equally, those lands shouldn't be solely the preserve of a privileged few to appreciate and enjoy.

Besides, we live in the 21st century and the idea that a first-born male heir can inherit huge swathes of Britain by virtue of his ancestor being mates with William the Conqueror, is quite frankly absurd.

Golden Wonder Winds the Church Clock and puts up the Flag

For me one of the things quintessentially British is the parish church: as communal hubs for millennia they, even in our secular age, link us to the past in a way that few other things can, and while I'm not particularly religious I appreciate their importance and enjoy my visits to them; the English ones in particular, because the Victorians reinstated stained glass and ornate screens making them aesthetically beautiful and easy on the eye.

Up and down the country a small irregular army of volunteers maintain and look after these places: unsung heroes who give up a portion of their free time each week to perform the routine tasks that occasional visitors such as myself generally take for granted. One such man is Ian Ferriday.

Ian, or Golden Wonder as he's affectionately known, is a former marathon runner who moved to Grasmere from Manchester over forty years ago to work and pursue his sporting interests. The determination and single-mindedness required for racing extended to other aspects of his life and his interests are both numerous and eclectic. Once a week he ascends the church tower at St Oswalds to wind the clock and last week I went along with him.

The spiral steps leading up the medieval tower are narrow and windowless, which makes it difficult to know where you are in relation to the building and it's not until we emerge on the platform behind the clock that you get a sense of scale.

The acoustics within the small chamber amplify sound and the whirs, clicks, wheels and chimes create a musical repertoire that is both hypnotic and reassuring in its regularity, like a heartbeat.

Ian winds the clock with a crank handle and the action reminds me of the opening scene from the seventies kids programme Camberwick Green where the guy winds down the credits by pulling the crank towards him then pushing it over making an arc of his body. It's a good ten minute work-out that left Ian unable to speak for a minute or two afterwards. We then moved up to the roof for a panoramic uncluttered view of the surrounding area.

At twilight we returned to hoist the flag for Easter Sunday. When I asked why we were doing it on Saturday night he said

'You know what folk are like round here – They'll be up and about early walking their dogs and going for papers and if the flag isn't flying there'll be complaints; but I'm buggered if I'm getting up at 5 o'clock in the morning to climb the tower so I put it up the night before when it's dark and this way they're none the wiser.'

Customs and traditions that have become diluted or obsolete, and pass unnoticed in our towns and cities are pronounced and upheld in these villages. It's part of the glue that binds people together.

In Search of the Golden Eagle with Mountain Man

Stewart Reekie, (mountain man) is a dry stone waller, a climber and keen bird watcher. Most of his days are spent out on the fells and it's fair to say he knows these mountains better than most: so when he offered to show me England's last remaining wild golden eagle it was an opportunity not to be missed.

Haweswater reservoir was built during the Great Depression of the 1930s. It forms a great tongue of black water, ringed by mountains and is one of the Lake District's most isolated places. The village of Mardale with its church and graveyard; pubs, shops and streets lie submerged beneath the lake and driving alongside you can't help feeling there's something missing: it's as though the ghosts of times past are willing their presence known to the traveller.

The only road running into the valley comes to an abrupt end at the head of the lake. Here we pulled in and began making our way on foot along the beck and up the fellside. Walking with Stewart is like going for a walk with a mountain goat: foot-sure and agile he rarely breaks step and his breath, unlike mine, was never laboured: he traverses the steepest slopes with the ease of a man walking down to the shops. I let him go on ahead catching up with him at a small tarn called Bleawater, where I proceeded to cough up half an ounce of Golden Virginia while he sat around eating candied ginger. Blea translates as grey: here the mountain's dark shadow prevents the sky ever mirroring itself in the water, which was black and still with a thin film of ice partially covering its surface. Once rested we continued up to Riggindale Straits emerging above the eyrie: the eagle's nest.

Stewart spotted him perched on a ledge on the facing cliff: solitary and majestic, the last of his kind, in this loneliest of outposts I couldn't help feeling a tinge of sadness that a bird that features so predominantly in our culture both in symbolism and art could have been reduced to just one.

He feeds mainly on carrion: red deer and crag-fast sheep that become trapped and die on the ledges provide a plentiful supply of food, but for nine years he's been alone. Each year he builds an eyrie and takes to the sky circling and calling for a mate: but it's a ghost dance; he is the last of his kind and short of the authorities introducing a female, which they seem reluctant to do, his line will die with him.

The wind stilled when the sun went down and the only sound was the throaty clack, clack of the ravens as we made our way off the ridge and walked down the valley. Stewart went on ahead but I didn't mind: I was preoccupied. When we got back to the car I asked him.

'How much is a golden eagle?'

The Only Thing Missing were the Grizzlies

Catherine Kay is the Education Officer at the Wordsworth Trust. She read Romantic literature at St Andrews and has an extensive knowledge along with a love and passion for her subject. Away from the museum she immerses herself in popular culture; reads Heat magazine and watches Made in Chelsea.

The kind of person you'd take your proofreading to. The kind of person you'd want on your quiz team.

We've been friends for many years and one warm sunny afternoon last October we took a trip down to Force Falls to watch the migrating salmon leap the cataract on their way to the spawning grounds.

You need to get your eye in. We arrived an hour or so after high tide and didn't have to wait long before we saw them, tentative at first, lifting their heads above water to check out the falls before making the great leap. Occasionally one would mistime its jump, landing in the boiling, foaming water at the base. It's a spectacle we associate with rivers in the Yukon or Nova Scotia, but here we were a few miles south of Kendal watching one of the greatest shows on earth – the only thing missing were the grizzlies.

Most creatures, humans being one of the few exceptions, have magnetized sensors in their bodies; an internal GPS that taps in to the earth's magnetic field, enabling them to accurately navigate empty skies, oceans and featureless plateaus over years and thousands of miles, returning, in the salmon's case, through the rivers and tributaries to the gravel pits where they were born four years earlier. The urge to reproduce is greater than the obstacles nature puts before them and they'll overcome seemingly insurmountable difficulties in order to return.

The Lake District National Park is a menagerie: indigenous animals such as deer, badgers and birds of prey are visible on an almost daily basis, but the sight of those big Atlantic salmon leaping the waterfall was something I neither anticipated nor expected. It really was quite special.

The salmon migrate in October. To get to Force Falls take the Hincaster turn off on the A590 and go down the cul-de-sac running parallel to the road and river for around 800 metres. The Falls are on the left beside a farmhouse. The salmon arrive around an hour or two after high tide in Morecambe Bay.

Song of the Wandering Aengus
By W.B.Yeats

I went out to the hazel wood,

Because a fire was in my head,

And cut and peeled a hazel wand,

And hooked a berry to a thread;

And when white moths were on the wing,

and moth-like stars were flickering out,

I dropped the berry in the stream

And caught a little silver trout.

When I had laid it on the floor
I went to blow the fire aflame.
But something rustled on the floor,
And some one called me by my name:
It had become a glimmering girl
With apple blossom in her hair
Who called me by my name and ran
And faded through the brightening air.

Though I am old with wandering
Through hollow lands and hilly lands,
I will find out where she has gone,
And kiss her lips and take her hands;
And walk among long dappled grass,
And pluck till time and times are done
The silver apples of the moon,
The golden apples of the sun.

A Right Royal Bird

Rick Martin is a Romany gypsy who blends his own fine teas and hires out rowing boats from his lakeside kiosk Faeryland, which is set in a sheltered inlet beyond the village. It is the most picturesque of places and I've wiled away many an idle moment there. The bay is protected from the worst of the weather by trees and two promontories of land that give a pincer effect separating it from the main body of the lake and through which you must pass to get into open water.

Each Spring Grasmere's resident mute swans Henry and Henrietta build a nest on the edge of the headland and while she sits quietly with her brood, he patrols the channel. He's a cantankerous, unpredictable old sod and passing through can be like navigating the Straits of Hormuz – anything can happen. The situation isn't helped by the shallows where the long-fingered weeds cling to the hull giving the effect of rowing through treacle and it's always with a sense of relief that you get through and out into deeper water without incident. I feel myself fortunate that, while I've often had him trail in my wake or glide alongside like a frigate, he's never actually had a go.

He finds canoeists particularly objectionable and has capsized a number of unsuspecting enthusiasts over the years by approaching at speed then flying low at them to knock them off balance. The poet Carola Luther, herself a keen canoeist, spent many hours out on the lake, but on occasion Rick had to place himself in a boat between her and Henry to allow her safe passage. Familiarity is no guarantee. He fears no one, this is his territory and the decision to let people pass is entirely at his discretion.

He's there as I write – regal and proud: policing the channel; casually scanning the lake and shoreline for his next victim.

Bachelors Buttons and Alfred's Cakes

Sally Hall plays the clarinet: she's also my boss who works as the Senior Guide at Dove Cottage where she deals with the day to day running of the house and gardens – where we often find ourselves working alongside each other. I tend to the grass, trees, paths and drains, while she plants and weeds the beds. Much of my time is spent alone dealing with the general estate and I've come to enjoy and appreciate the times we spend together in the D.C garden.

The Wordsworths created the garden over two hundred years ago. They believed that when gardening you should work within the spirit of nature, with the invisible hand of art: it should be subtle not ostentatious. It's a principle and philosophy we try to adhere to today.

In many ways it's harder to make a garden look natural than it is to make it cultivated just as equally there's a very fine line between natural and unkempt. It's something we're very much aware of and try not to cross. Sally knows the names of all the flowers and I've always appreciated how imaginative people were in naming them: Bachelors Buttons, Dogtooth Violets, Turks Cap Lilies, Lady's Mantle etc. The colloquial names are far more vivid and sensual than the Latin, which I always forget.

A stretch of woodland lies on the far side of the perimeter wall and the other day while out checking the deer fence I came across a cluster of combustible mushrooms called Alfred's Cakes. Bulbous or conical in shape with a scorched appearance they form in clusters on dead ash trees. They are remarkable in that when dried and lit they can retain heat for up to four hours. Ancient nomadic people placed them in horns and used them to carry fire between camps. They burn from within like a coal; blowing on it turns it into a glowing ember that can be used to start another fire.

It never ceases to amaze me how resourceful our ancestors were.

Man is Born Free and Everywhere He is in Chains

This time last year the Treasury sent out a self-congratulatory tweet announcing that millions of us had helped end the slave trade through our taxes. The 184-year loan, taken out by the government in 1833 to pay out slave owners to end slavery, had finally been paid off and we'd all played a part.

The tweet was quickly deleted when the Caribbean community reacted to the realisation they'd been paying off the people that had enslaved their ancestors.

David Cameron's ancestor benefited to the tune of around three million quid from the pay-out. Lacking self-awareness, he visited Jamaica as Prime Minister and offered to build them a prison. He wanted to transport Jamaicans held in British prisons back to Jamaica to be locked up there. Shipping people across the Atlantic in chains? The irony was lost on Dave.

Dave's ignorance of his own family history and his general recklessness, highlight a much bigger issue. We don't have great leaders.

The Greeks understood that democracy was always going to be flawed, because we ourselves are. Know Thyself, written on the temple of Apollo at Delphi was the best advice they could give.

Notably absent from Boris's lexicon of Classical quotes, it asks us to re-examine ourselves – to seek the answers within.

Personally, I'm tired of false prophets and snake-oil sellers peddling El Dorado. Using the lowest common denominator – an existential fear of immigrants, refugees and foreigners in general – to garner support. I'm seeking the remarkable in the ordinary and I've always found my heroes closer to home.

Around here, you can find your Gandhis and your Amy Johnsons in the local store. They're easy to spot. The one who takes his own path, has taken his trolley in the opposite direction to everyone else and caused a traffic jam in the coffee aisle. Bloody pioneers! Companies spend fortunes profiling us and designing stores so that we behave and shop in a certain way. Namely, buying a load of stuff we didn't realise we wanted and probably don't need. We're being manipulated and don't even notice it most of the time. But they can't factor in the mavericks. Regular shoppers' frown on their behaviour, but I'm reassured; they give me hope. Not everyone's conforming to type.

Small acts can make big statements. Like the guy who picked up a piece of red ochre and drew a picture on the cave wall. The one who melted some sand and created a window through which to view the world. They weren't bound by convention, they thought for themselves and for the greater good. All great revolutions start with a small act of defiance. We don't have to follow each other blindly. It's important to remember that it's our curiosity that has enabled us to evolve.

A Long Way from Kingston

Our taste for exotic and alternative food isn't new. Curry was a popular dish in this country in the late eighteenth / early nineteenth centuries: the first vegetarian restaurants also opened around that time, but it didn't last; going out of fashion in the Victorian period and becoming popular again in my lifetime.

David Wilson grew up in Manchester's Moss Side, a predominantly West Indian suburb south of the city centre, where he developed a taste and passion for their culture and cuisine, which stayed with him when he moved to Blackburn twenty-five years ago. He loves cooking and his exuberance is infectious: he's had a number of cafes over the years before opening Calypso, a Caribbean restaurant at Eanam Wharf; a former warehouse beside the Leeds Liverpool canal, where I went along to meet him. I'd assumed we'd be sitting around a table having a chat and taking notes, but I should've known better – David has a reggae boat: we climbed aboard, started the engine, switched on the speakers and spent the next hour or so cruising up and down the canal.

At 127 miles the Leeds Liverpool is the longest canal in the country. Begun in 1770, war and local politics delayed its construction and it wasn't completed until 1816. With access to the port of Liverpool and the coalfields of East Lancashire and

West Yorkshire towns like Blackburn mushroomed with factories and warehouses lining its route, some of which, though long derelict, are still visible today. David pointed out the old police station with the rusted bars of the cells still fixed in the wall just above water level. Here, petty criminals would be held prior to being loaded onto barges and taken to Liverpool for transportation to the penal colonies. Next to the police station are the remains of the bank: its money chute, now home to a family of pigeons.

As a native of the town the canal also courses through my veins and I found myself journeying back to my own childhood: being warned to stay away from the black water because Ginny Greenteeth lived there and drew in children who strayed too close to the edge; walking with a sweetheart down the towpath and stealing a kiss beneath one of its many bridges. A local legend, Spring Heeled Jack was said to have jumped across the canal. Witnesses record how his foot touched down in the middle and without breaking the surface tension he sprang onto the opposite bank. It was noted on examination that the sole of his right boot was wet.

The decision to build broad locks allowed the canal to compete with the railway for trade and it continued to carry coal and aggregates up until the 1970s: its demise coinciding with the decline of the manufacturing industries across the region.

These days the canal is given over to pleasure craft, and former warehouses such as Eanam Wharf, which were once storage depots for goods and raw materials from America and the West Indies have been adapted for today's needs. Geographically, Calypso may be a long way from Kingston but in terms of the building's history, it's almost on the doorstep.

Dem Bones, Dem Bones

The searchlight followed her, and a shudder ran through all who saw her, for lashed to the helm was a corpse, with drooping head, which swung horribly to and fro at each motion of the ship. No other form could be seen on deck at all. A great awe came on all as they realised that the ship, as if by a miracle, had found the harbour, unsteered save by the hands of a dead man...There was of course a considerable concussion as the vessel drove up on the sand-heap. Every spar, rope, and stay was strained, and some of the 'top-hammer' came crashing down. But, strangest of all, the very instant the shore was touched, an immense dog sprang up on deck from below, as if shot up by the concussion, and running forward, jumped from the bow on to the sand. Making straight for the steep cliff, where the churchyard hangs over the laneway to the East Pier so steeply that some of the flat tombstones – 'thruff-steans' or 'through-stones', as they call them in the Whitby vernacular – actually project over where the sustaining cliff has fallen away, it disappeared in the darkness, which seemed intensified just beyond the focus of the searchlight.

From *Dracula* by Bram Stoker

I've recently returned from Whitby: a busy little port on the north east coast with a long and illustrious history. It's one of the finest little towns in the north of England and one I've revisited each year with Annalie for the past three Spring / Summers.

The ruined abbey on the cliff, the white-walled fishermen's cottages with their orange tiled roofs and the blue sky punctuated by crying gulls and tolling church bells, help make it a perfect writers retreat.

It's also a palaeontologists dream with regular rockslides revealing the fossil record of the inhabitants of long-dead oceans. Even for amateurs such as ourselves a stroll along the beach reveals fragments of ammonites, crinoids and nautiloids that lived on the seabed millions of years ago.

St Mary's churchyard, where parts of Dracula take place, sits adjacent to the abbey, and the sandstone monuments to the dead – weathered and honeycombed by wind and rain – ease out from the church to the edge of the cliffs. Last winter severe storms brought down a section of cliff above the town and with it part of the churchyard. Carried down and scattered by the landslide, many of the bones ended up at the back of Fortune's Kippers smokehouse. It's as though the dead, no longer content to lie around and wait to be petrified, have burst out from their underground chambers to dally once more among the living. The Goths will love it…

The church itself, where Captain Cook attended as an apprentice sailor, is an architectural wonder: large boxed family pews dominate the nave surrounded on all sides by tiered public galleries raised on columns high above. Large inscribed tablets fixed to the walls remind people of the perils of ignorance and the glory of God.

The early nineteenth century saw an evangelical revival and sermons could last for hours. In the 1820s the Reverend James Andrews fixed two large ear trumpets to the side of the pulpit so that his long suffering wife, who had mercifully gone deaf, could be perched at the base and plugged in. A gesture he no-doubt believed would bring her salvation.

The dog in the picture isn't really Dracula. It's Jasmine from Tweedies Bar posing for her picture in Grasmere churchyard.

The Cloths of Gold

Traditionally the Lake District's economy was sustained by farming and heavy industry. Wool, heavy metals, slate, coal and graphite were processed here and exported around the country and beyond, but these days, for the most part, tourism has replaced these traditional industries and Grasmere vale, which in Wordsworth's time sustained twenty-five farms and two quarries has been reduced to just four farms. That said, while the small-scale nature of much of what I've mentioned make them economically unviable in the modern age the artisan crafts associated with them continue to thrive albeit on a much smaller scale. We've retained a blacksmith, stonemasons and until recently a Master handloom weaver in the larger than life form of Malcolm Reekie.

Malcolm 'Malie' comes from a family of Master weavers who moved to Grasmere from Selkirk not long after the war to work in a weaving shed in the village. It was the beginnings of commercial tourism and seeing an opportunity his father set up his own business in the old slaughterhouse up the Easdale valley – which proved hugely successful allowing him to construct a purpose built workshop on the edge of the village.

Malcolm started work in a quarry at the age of sixteen: three years later he became apprenticed to his father and began to learn the trade before eventually taking over the business when his father retired.

In Grasmere no two days are the same: the light is constantly changing and with it the colours and mood. Malcolm used this as his palette and began creating pieces that mirrored the surrounding fells in their dramatic beauty and ever changing tones. Word soon spread and he began receiving orders from all over the world. A piece called Autumn Gold was presented to Princess Anne on her wedding day: other notables followed including Princess Margaret and the Maharaja of Jaipur.

He retired at sixty to indulge in more leisurely pursuits. These days the yarn he spins are the stories of his own eventful life and I often meet up with him at Tweedies. He's a jovial fellow, quick to laugh with an easy smile and I've spent many a pleasant hour or two in his company.

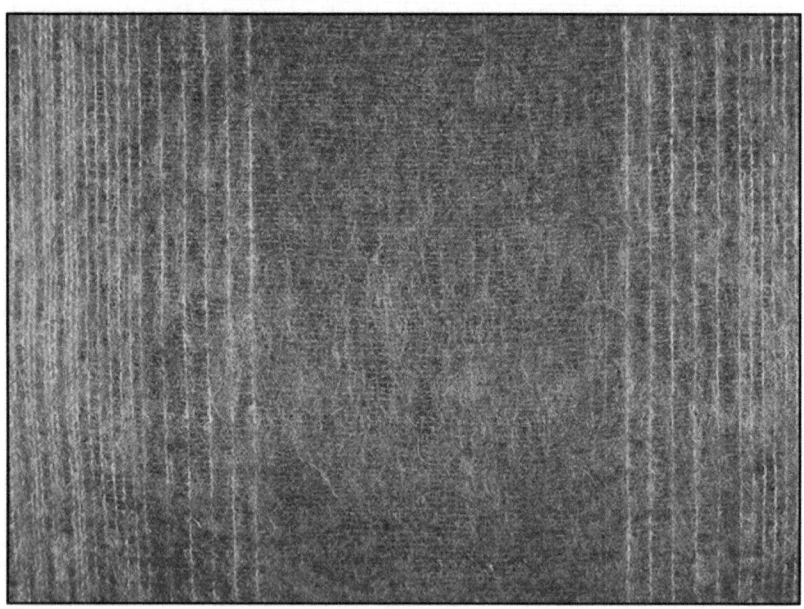

Statistically Speaking

Over 40% of the houses in Grasmere are holiday homes, most of which sit empty through the Winter. In Elterwater it's around 85%: no longer a living village, just obstacles to manoeuvre around on your way to somewhere else. In many cases the cottages were sold on by the offspring of villagers who themselves moved out to the churchyards. Many of the properties, quaint as holiday lets, were deemed too isolated, primitive and impractical for modern family living. The high prices help of course...

Tony Sanderson is a third generation Grasmerian. He and Mo have been married thirty-two years – part of the sixty percent that make Grasmere a living village. They, like a lot of my friends, don't have kids and in many ways the bond between them is stronger as a result. They enjoy each other's company and hang out and holiday together like a couple of old friends – which they are.

It was that fact that so many professional people are choosing not to have children that got me thinking about the future of the human race – as you do. So I began to look at the statistics beginning with what was a generally misconceived belief that there are more people alive than have ever died.

We don't get an accurate census until AD 1800 when the population stood at around one billion. Using this as a guide the Washington Institute for Population Studies, beginning with the emergence of homo sapiens 50,000 years ago and a population of two and including the current population of seven billion, estimates that 107 billion have died: meaning each one of us carries fifteen ghosts behind us.

The current rate of twenty-three births per thousand population differs greatly from the eighty births per thousand in ancient times. The current rate wouldn't have sustained the species when life expectancy was much lower.

I then began to look at extinction rates. Only 0.1% of species that have ever lived are still alive. 99.9% are extinct. A successful species can expect to survive up to ten million years; though that is the exception.

It doesn't look too good for us, but then you have to put things in perspective. We've only been around 50,000 years: two thousand years ago Caesar was hanging out with Cleopatra and ten million years is a long time.

I suppose what I'm really saying is, that it's all going to end sometime so whatever lifestyle you choose, make the most of it.

Ancestors

By Neil Rollinson

We all without a single exception inherit
all our genes from an unbroken line
of successful ancestors
Richard Dawkins.

When I reach for you in the hot night
I wonder, do I really want you,
or are my genes on fire for some distant shore?

As we fuck in the night, I can hear them singing,
choir to choir in the endless dark.
I think of our ancestors, the distance
they travelled – out of the slime
and into the trees, through the ice ages
and the shifting of continents.
They came through plagues that wasted millions,
hunger, poverty, war. Not one of them
failed to find a mate. They slipped through aeons
passing their code from body to body,
to me and you in the distant future,
a childless couple drinking beer,
talking politics and science. To think
it all ends here for these particular passengers,
to have come this far and found a blank. If I were
the sentimental type
I'd take you now in the alley behind the bar,
and do the honourable thing.
I'd open the floodgates and let them go,
screaming and singing into the future.

Divisions

The Solway Firth forms a natural border between England and Scotland. Over ten miles wide at its mouth, it narrows to a patchwork of marshland and estuaries where the rivers Esk and Eden flow into the sea, and which can be forded at low tide through the spring and summer months. It's a quiet corner of England, bypassed by commerce and the tourist hoards who prefer the picturesque setting of the South Lakes or the highlands and islands of Scotland and yet its story, still visible along the coastline records two defining moments in our nations' history.

In AD 121 the Roman Emperor Hadrian visited Britain, as part of a tour aimed at containing and consolidating his vast empire. He marked the outer limit with the construction of a series of forts and a wall stretching from Bowness on Solway to the northeast coast, separating the Scots and Picts from the northern Celtic tribes. A remarkable piece of engineering, it also made a statement of division both psychological and physical which would have the effect of creating two nations on one small island.

On the marshland a quarter mile from the small village of Burgh by Sands, a large sandstone monument marks the spot where King Edward I, aged and debilitated by dysentery, died while leading his army into Scotland.

Edward I 'Longshanks' was an imposing man. Standing 6'2' tall he epitomized medieval kingship. A strong ruler and lawgiver, a fearless soldier and devout Christian, he left his mark on our country as few other monarchs have. He brought stability to the fractious feudal realm he inherited, upheld and enshrined in law the principles of Magna Carta, and created the modern constituency-based parliament. He was equally pious and generous, intimidating and cruel; and it's through his subjugation of the Welsh princes and his wars in Scotland that he remains such a divisive figure to this day – especially north of the border.

One popular story of his death tells of him requesting that his body be boiled and his flesh stripped from the bones, which were to be placed in a casket and carried at the head of the army on future invasions of Scotland. It goes on to say that his son, the future Edward II, ignored his request burying him at Westminster Abbey with the Latin epithet 'Hammer of the Scots' inscribed on his tomb. It's a good story, but it isn't true.

Knowing his son to be weak and fearful for his kingdom, he summoned the barons to discuss the accession and future of the realm. On his death he was taken to the nearby church of St Michael's where he was embalmed, and lay in state surrounded by his royal standards for ten days before being taken on a slow procession to London. He was interred at the abbey in a plain tomb bearing only his coat of arms. The inscription: *Edwardus Primus Scottorum Malleus, hic est 1308 Pactum Serva.* Here lies Edward I, Hammer of the Scots. Keep the Vow; was added in the 16th century.

Fearing a counter-invasion, news of his death was suppressed with severe penalties imposed on anyone who talked. When word eventually filtered through, Robert the Bruce brought his army across the marsh; passing the stone cairn marking the place where the king died, and exacted his bloody revenge on the towns and villages along the coast. Even the monastery at Holm Cultram (Abbeytown) where his father is buried wasn't spared.

Hadrian's border issues, Edward's megalomania, Robert the Bruce's revenge. It's a small place with a big story and well worth a visit if you're in the area.

From Thomas Gray's' ***The Bard – A Pindaric Ode'***

Ruin seize thee, ruthless king!
Confusion on thy banners wait,
Though fanned by Conquest's crimson wing
They mock the air with idle state.
Helm nor hauberk's twisted mail,
Nor even thy virtues, tyrant, shall avail
To save thy secret soul from nightly fears,
From Cambria's curse, from Cambria's tears!'
Such were the sounds, that o'er the crested pride
Of the first Edward scattered wild dismay,
As down the steep of Snowdon's shaggy side
He wound with toilsome march his long array.

Blackburn Blues

I've just returned from Blackburn: my hometown and a place we'll revisit a number of times over the course of this blog. My parents, grandparents and generations of my family lie in its cemeteries. Tim and Jules, my eldest and younger brothers live there along with a close network of friends I can happily get drunk with, or sit around drinking coffee depending on the time of day. We share each other's triumphs and disasters and one day we'll carry each other's coffins. It's that kind of place, and while my home and many of my friends are here in Grasmere my roots are firmly embedded in the sand and clay of East Lancashire.

Jules Ward is a singer/songwriter: a rhythm and blues man he moved back to Blackburn with his family a couple of years ago from Berlin, where he lived and played the blues for thirteen years, gigging in the all-night bars and flipping burgers at the Hard Rock Café to pay the rent.

Towns like Blackburn embraced and gave themselves over to subversive music: raw angry punk: low down dirty blues and briefly acid house all found an audience and an outlet in the bars, clubs and, in the case of acid house, the disused Victorian factories where the broken glass and pigeon shit ground to paste beneath the revellers' feet and a hollow dawn, tinctured with the smell of stale sweat and yeast, greeted the emerging party.

The environment we grow up in shapes us in many different ways. Jules began playing drums in a punk band before picking up the guitar at the age of fifteen. He's been a troubadour for almost thirty years playing in Berlin, Prague, Warsaw and Copenhagen along with a stint in Cuba, Central America and North America's west coast. He once told me that I should have continued playing; he said

'You're never lonely when you have a guitar. If you feel down you pick it up, play a few tunes, and you feel good about yourself again.' He is a true exponent of his craft.

The Beggar's Banquet

It's getting like New Delhi around here for begging and street sleeping. Unprecedented in my lifetime; on busy shopping days they line the routes like sitting Buddhas, creating eddies in the pedestrian traffic as it tos-and-fros along the streets; and it's rare that I can get through the town without giving away a cigarette, or some money for the bus, a cup of tea, some food, whatever. It creates a dilemma because while I want to help, even consider it a moral duty, to assist those in need; at the same time, I don't want to be screwed over. The dilemma's in part because begging and homelessness are two different issues: not all beggars are desperate and homeless; and equally, not all desperate, homeless people beg.

When it comes to vocational begging, you'd be hard pushed to beat the woman who recently appeared on my little shopping street. Swinging up the pavement on a pair of crutches with a squashed empty Weetabix box under her arm, she sat on the doorstep by the One Stop entrance begging money for milk for her cereal. The slight flaw in the ruse was that along with making a few quid, she ended up with about ten pints of milk which she tried unsuccessfully to sell to the shop across the street. She was obliged to purchase two carrier bags and hobbled awkwardly away, weighted down with cartons of milk. Undeterred, she returned a couple of days later, this time asking for money for milk as they exited the shop, thereby avoiding the literal interpretation of the question.

She's a complete charlatan, amusing in a perverse kind of way, the problem is people like her can generate a cynicism among the giving public and the genuine people who do need help end up losing out.

When it comes to charity, the act of giving can call into question our own motives. Are we doing it in an altruistic sense? Or, to make us feel better about ourselves? The answer of course, is both. The poet William Wordsworth put it succinctly in his poem *The Old Cumberland Beggar*. A polemic against a group of politicians, lobbying the Government to tighten the vagrancy laws.

`But deem not this man useless – Statesmen! Ye
Who are so restless in your wisdom, ye
Who have a broom still ready in your hands
To rid the world of nuisances…
While thus he creeps
From door to door, the Villagers in him
Behold a record which together binds
Past deeds and offices of charity
Else unremembered, and so keeps alive
The kindly mood in hearts…´

Wordsworth has the beggar as benefactor; a custodian of kindnesses bestowed upon him. Rekindled when they next see him, the villagers remember their past generosity and it makes them feel good about themselves, resulting in both parties gaining from the transaction in a mutually beneficial way.

Of course, we have to assume that Wordsworth's beggar wasn't looking to buy some cans of strong lager and a bag of Spice with the proceeds – or the equivalent of. But even if he was, does it matter, when the gift has returned such a gift?

No homeless person ever aspired to sleeping on the street, but some have fallen further than others to get there.

I met Little Damien when I was in my late teens. He was a softly spoken guy with a genuine warmth about him. For over twenty-five years he worked as an auxiliary/driver for the NHS at various mental health units. Around fifteen years ago he had a breakdown, hit the booze and everything fell apart. In a short space of time he lost his job, his family, his house and his money. With no fixed address and unable, or incapable of claiming benefits he ended up destitute, living in a shared dormitory in a flea-pit hostel in the centre of town. The accommodation was night-time only and each interminably long day was spent wandering the streets.

When I saw him again for the first time, I was shocked. His hair and beard were long and matted and his layers of mis-matched clothing were dirty and threadbare. He lowered his gaze when he saw me, and I ashamedly did the same, embarrassed for myself and for him. We passed without acknowledging each other. It was a cowardly thing to do and I didn't feel too good about myself afterwards.

Damien didn't beg, he retained that level of dignity, but he would accept if offered. I last saw him a year before he died. We sat on a wall and smoked a couple of cigarettes. His eye had retained its softness throughout his tribulations. He was still the same kind, gentle man I'd met all those years before. There was no embarrassment between us, just acceptance.

He was found floating in the canal one morning in late February. News of his death brought on a lot of soul-searching from those of us who knew him, but ultimately, I at least concluded, we were as helpless as he was.

In another time there would've been safety nets for people like Damien in the form of care and social housing – as you would expect for a man who had worked and paid into the system throughout his adult life – but sadly that's no longer the case. Having first forced our Councils to sell off their housing stock, the government then went for the jugular and hacked social services. The foundations that support us and the glue that binds it all together, the post-war blue-print for a fairer more equal society, has been erased and the effects are to be found in the doorways and underpasses of our towns and cities.

It's no good simply building houses for people who can afford to buy them. We need to build houses so that people can have somewhere to live. To allow them that quiet dignity. In a rich country such as ours it shouldn't be too much to ask.

High Tides and Shifting Sands

The tidal bore that emerges from the Lune Deeps at the mouth of Morecambe Bay is said to run faster than a galloping horse, flooding the channels that cut through the sand silently and rapidly in minutes. It's deceptive and lethal, with the graveyards and memorials around the bay bearing testament to its speed and unforgiving nature.

Patches of quicksand that can shift a hundred metres in as many hours; coupled with weather systems than can give the effect of turning the bay into a washing machine, add to its unpredictability.

It's also one of the most exhilarating places to be and last weekend I, along with my colleagues Jane, Esther and Catherine, joined Alan Sledmore and Jack for a nine-mile guided cross bay walk from Hest Bank to Grange over Sands.

Jane Connolly, Esther Rutter and Catherine Harland make up part of the Wordsworth Trust's permanent staff. They are firm friends and we've known and worked alongside each other in various capacities for over four years. They are graduates of Leeds, Oxford and Durham respectively and are great fun to work with, and hang out with socially. Prior to setting out, I was bit concerned about their fitness levels (they'll kill me for this), but needn't have worried as they made the crossing with the agility and grace of gazelles.

Before the road and rail networks connected what's now South West Cumbria with Lancashire, travellers wishing to make the journey north / south took the treacherous route across the sands, but these days, fisher folk aside, the trip is made purely for pleasure and we set out with a hundred or so fellow pilgrims and what seemed like half of the local fishing community, as back up, to make the crossing.

Jack has the look of a man who has spent all his life on the sands: red faced and sporting a bandana he reads them and knows their ways. He's also a great character and a reassuring presence on such a long and arduous crossing. The ever changing nature of the bay make no two days the same and while I personally have made the journey on a number of occasions we've never taken the same route twice, making each experience unique.

We'd been walking for an hour or so when we came upon an island that had reappeared this year after the winter storms. It had lain buried for over eighty years re-emerging overnight with its century old nets and fish traps still intact. Jack informed us that they'd begun to catch fish again, though the channel the nets had once faced had moved ninety degrees to the right in the decades since the island vanished beneath the sands.

Four hours after setting out we reached our destination; tired and windswept, but with a sense of achievement that we'd made the crossing safely and without incident. We dried ourselves off and put on our boots to walk the few hundred metres to the station, to board the waiting coaches that would take us back to our starting point. Half an hour later the channels were full and the bay was once again beginning to flood.

A Sorry End

John Dixon was a publisher, author and historian who, in the spirit of notable Blackburn writers Alfred Wainwright and Jessica Lofthouse created a series of historic walks through the Lancashire countryside that have engaged and delighted countless people over the past twenty five years. He was my good friend and publisher who sadly died suddenly late last year. When it came to the area around east Lancashire he was a walking encyclopaedia and you'd be hard pushed to find a more eloquent and interesting companion for a stroll in the countryside. One day he took me to see the last resting place of Jeppe Knave.

Pendle Hill is an iconic Lancashire landmark that rises out of the Ribble valley like a misshaped loaf. Its association with the witch trials of 1612 has given it a legendary status, but its human history pre-dates written records by a few thousand years and is still visible if you know where to look, in the form of Megalithic and Neolithic settlements and cawhamber tombs. In one such grave lies Jeppe Knave.

The 1320s were a turbulent period in England. A weak king in Edward II had allowed the barons to consolidate their power and the north of the country was terrorised and laid siege to by reivers from the Scottish borders. The resulting chaos left large areas virtually lawless; roamed by gangs of renegades led by men who murdered and robbed at will and with seeming impunity. One such man was Jeppe Knave.

England in the fourteenth century was a devoutly catholic country and the belief that the sins of this life would be judged in the next encouraged a culture of fear and superstition. The dying received Confession and after death were placed in consecrated ground, facing east, in anticipation of the Day of Judgement. It was important to be buried in one piece as missing bits had to be sought out prior to appearing before God. In the poem 'Relic' by John Donne the bereaved spouse carries to his grave a bracelet made from his dead lover's hair, that she might seek him out in the afterlife.

A bracelet of bright hair about the bone,

Will he not let us alone,

And think that there a loving couple lies,

Who thought that this device might be some way
To make their souls, at the last busy day,
Meet at this grave, and make a little stay?

The wealthy built Chantry Chapels and paid for mass to be said daily to ease them through purgatory, while the poor prayed to saints.

Jeppe Knave was captured then taken to a pagan place on the west of Pendle, where he was beheaded and thrown into an ancient chamber tomb. The message was clear: there would be no redemption; by this act he'd been consigned to Hell for all eternity. Sometime later a cross was carved into one of the stones and in more recent times his name was crudely added.

Returning here to write this blog I'm struck by the grave's complete isolation; far from the main footpaths and known only to a few it nevertheless depicts the beliefs and customs of two remarkable periods in our turbulent history.

From **Inferno**
By Dante Alighieri

But fix your eyes on that valley, we are approaching
The river of blood in which everyone boils
Who does harm to his neighbour by violence.
***
Around the ditch they [Centaurs] go, thousand after thousand,
Loosing arrows at any spirit which rises
Further out of the blood than its guilt allows.
***
Then we moved on with our faithful escort,
Along the edge of the boiling red liquid,
From which came the shrill cries of the scalded.

The Italian Job

The twisted road that snakes itself over the pass isn't for the faint hearted. Impassable for much of the winter it's a gravity-defying ascent that tests your engine and your nerve as you make your way up and over the summit. From there the valley of Eskdale with its scattered farms and patchwork fields runs out into the sea. On a raised rocky plateau a couple of hundred metres from the road stands Hardknott Roman fort. Built by the emperor Hadrian in the 2nd century AD, its complete isolation, far from any settlements has kept its structure intact. It is one of the best-preserved Roman ruins in Britain, and the other day I went along with Kat and Susan to check it out.

Katherine Wynn and Susan Leedham studied English literature at Lancaster and U.E.A respectively, and Susan completed a Masters at Leeds. They are part of the Wordsworth Trust's award winning trainee programme that each year takes some of the brightest graduates from around the country, to work as part of the curatorial team for a year, before moving on to museums and galleries around the country. The yearly rotation is one of the reasons the Trust is so dynamic and vibrant for both visitors and the permanent staff who work alongside the trainees on a daily basis.

Hadrian came to Britain in AD121 and spent almost two years here, during which time he embarked on a number of defensive projects in order to define and protect his empire. Hardknott was one in a series of forts linking the port of Ravenglass with the city of York. Built on a three and a half acre site overlooking the river Esk it commands a clear uninterrupted view across the valley. The perimeter walls are two metres high and almost as thick, with turrets at each corner and four gates facing north, south, east and west. Inside the fort the remains of the headquarters building, the granaries and the commandant's house are still visible while outside the fort stand the circular bathhouse / sauna and the parade ground. An inscribed stone found at the site reads: 'For the emperor Caesar Trajanus Hadrianus Augustus… the fourth cohort of Dalmatians made this.'

Before leaving Britain Hadrian personified the country as a goddess and had a shrine dedicated to her at York. Coins were also minted bearing her likeness. She was called Britannia.

A Brief History of the Alehouse

'You can't sit there.'

I'd just got a pint at the Corporation and was about to sit down in the corner chair.

'Why not?' I said a bit perplexed.

'That's Albert's seat.'

'There's no-one here,' I said pointing to the empty bar.

'Never mind about that, and less of your cheek – he'll be in shortly.'

In my younger days 'the local' was just that, and the regulars had their own chairs that were reserved, as I discovered, whether they were around or not.

Beer has been brewed in this country since the Bronze Age, but it wasn't until the Romans arrived and built a convenient network of roads that the first public houses appeared, beginning a tradition that has continued uninterrupted for two thousand years. It is an integral part of our culture that has featured and been celebrated in song, literature and art. Chaucer's characters begin their pilgrimage to Canterbury at the Tabard Inn in Southwark, and John Barleycorn, a folk song in which barley itself is personified appeared around the same time. In the seventeenth century version below, three drunks try to kill the barley, by way of revenge.

There was three men come out o' the west their fortunes for to try,
And these three men made a solemn vow, John Barleycorn must die,
They ploughed, they sowed, they harrowed him in, throwed clods upon his head,
And these three men made a solemn vow, John Barleycorn was dead.

Robert Burns' poem *Tam O' Shanter,* begins with Tam getting merrily drunk at the market tavern while his wife sits at home quietly seething, in a scene familiar to many.

Gathering her brows like gathering storm
Nursing her wrath to keep it warm

Alex Goodall is the manager of the family run Tweedies Bar, a CAMRA listed pub that specialises in real ale and locally produced food here in Grasmere. Outside of work it acts as our village community centre where we can meet up and swap stories at the end of the week. The name Goodall comes from good ale and is an old English name that was given to brewers and landlords in the middle-ages. Many of the people I've written about on this blog frequent the pub and while we do have a regulars' corner, unlike Ken's customers at the Corporation, we don't have reserved seats. Alex is an affable host: well-travelled and a keen snowboarder, when he's not serving customers he's a customer himself, joining the rest of us in the corner or sitting with friends in the beer garden.

The eighty or so lakes and tarns that give the area its name make it a perfect place for brewing and along with the larger well established companies, many small micro-breweries operate within or alongside the National Park, sustained by local shops and pubs that provide an outlet and an income for their products. Each September Tweedies hosts the Grasmere Guzzler beer festival where over eighty beers and ciders are on offer. Alex's brother Jim operates the hog roasts and live music is performed throughout the weekend making it one of the highlights on the autumn calendar.

Now You See It

Pareidolia is a Greek word for the psychological condition that causes us to see faces in objects. The phenomena originates from an inbuilt survival instinct, activated at birth that allows us to recognise the human face in a fraction of a second and determine that person's intentions towards us. The side effect of this ability to distinguish friend or foe from a distance is that it causes us to see faces in trees, clouds, and countless inanimate objects, including hills and mountains. The other day I went along with Dean to check a couple of them out.

Dean Hines obtained his degree at Goldsmiths College before attending Portsmouth University where he completed an MA in art history. He works in heritage retail at the Wordsworth Trust and has a keen interest in art and literature. He's currently working on a historical novel and can often be found down at Tweedies with a pint and his notebook. He's also an accomplished pianist. When I told him of my plan to inspect a couple of these places, he was happy to come along with me.

Wild Boar Fell is in the Howgills, a range of fells bordering Eastern Cumbria and the Yorkshire Dales. Sweeping up from the Eden valley they form a dramatic backdrop against the fertile river wended vale. Six miles south of the market village of Kirkby

Stephen stand the ruins of Uther Pendragon's castle, an early Norman structure allegedly built on the site of King Arthur's father's house. In the twelfth century Sir Hugh de Morville, Lord of Westmoreland, occupied it. He was one of the four knights who murdered Thomas Beckett, and, after initially fleeing to France, took refuge there.

He was a troubled man – haunted at night by the moonlight on Wild Boar Fell: its outline bearing an uncanny resemblance to the face and mitre of the murdered archbishop.

Closer to home stands Stone Arthur an anthropomorphic peak that from certain angles resembles the reposing king. Like Wales and Cornwall the area possesses a strong Celtic tradition. The mountains Helvellyn and Blencathra, the rivers Derwent and Eden along with the town of Penrith, retain their names from that early period. The legend of Arthur is also strong here. Aside from the castle there is Arthur's Round Table, a Bronze Age earth ring at Eamont Bridge where the king is said to have held council. Close by is the Giants' Cave where Tarquin and Isir devoured human flesh. The poet Tennyson was convinced that Excalibur was in one of the lakes and composed his poem King Arthur while staying at Mire House on the shores of Bassenthwaite Lake.

The legends tell of him being a good king. Our benign Stone Arthur here in Grasmere is waiting, as the story goes, for the day when the country is in dire peril, and then he will rise again and come to our assistance.

Weights and Measures

In the *Book of Daniel*, King Belshazzar, having trampled his foes and trashed their temple, held a great feast to celebrate his victory. When the party was in full swing, the hand of God appeared, and as the King and guests looked on in horror and amazement, it began to write on the wall. The message proclaimed that the King's days were numbered. He had been *weighed and measured, and had been found wanting.*

His unsuitability to rule had been exposed and his fate was sealed.

At the Palace of Westminster, Boris Johnson, having trampled his principles and his colleagues, is, we are told, assured victory in the leadership race. The man who would be King, is about to get the top job. The champagne's on ice and the banqueting hall is being prepared. With the absence of a divine scribe, or graffiti artist, as we'd call them today, and with many people having serious reservations about his suitability, I thought I'd take this opportunity to weigh and measure him here and see how he shapes up.

We all know Boris is a character, but to quote a line from *Pulp Fiction*. "Just because you are a character, doesn't mean you have character."

Boris studied the Classics, so we'll give a heads-up to them as we go.

The Roman Empire covered much of Western Europe, North Africa and the Middle East. It had a common rule of law and in exchange for loyalty it guaranteed security and citizens' rights. It also allowed for the free movement of goods, services and people, within its borders.

Sound familiar?

When the Empire collapsed, we were left isolated and vulnerable. The country slid into economic decline, beset by internal squabbles and the constant threat of invasion. In the fear and uncertainty people found themselves yearning for the stability, peace and prosperity they'd once known.

For seventy years Europe has been at peace with itself. Its strength lies in its unity, which has allowed it to co-exist and collectively prosper, economically and socially to the benefit of all of its citizens. That unity is now being tested and it's in no small part down to Boris, who surprised both his friends and colleagues by switching from a pro-EU stance to a Leave one, in the space of three days. Lending his fame and giving heavyweight political clout to the Leave campaign, he undoubtedly helped swing the vote. This is Boris in June 2016.

BJ. *"This is a market on our doorstep, ready for further exploitation by British firms. The membership fee seems rather small for all that access. Why are we so determined to turn our back on it?"*

This was an article written for his Telegraph column in June 2016. It wasn't published as a few days later he surprised everyone by switching sides.

And from his friend and colleague Sir Nicholas Soames, grandson of Winston Churchill.

"Whatever my great friend Boris decides to do I know that he is NOT an outer."

Privately, his colleagues said that it was his personal ambitions, rather than his beliefs and convictions, that had swung him.

On the campaign trail he went all Marie Antoinette, banging on about us 'having our cake and eating it.'

It was all a game; he was having fun. It didn't matter because he never imagined he would win, as was evident the morning of the referendum result when a visibly shocked Boris appeared to the gathered media. *"We're still European"*, he stuttered, almost apologetically, having realised the magnitude of his actions. A Pyrrhic Victory? He'd won, but at what cost?

He'd rubbed the lamp and released the genie. There was no going back.

Still, there was no point him allowing a National crisis, partly of his making, to get in the way of his career. There was a leadership contest to contend and he was a frontrunner, only for his Brexit pal Michael Gove to do the 'Roman thing' and stab him in the back! "Et tu, Brute", quipped his dad, upon hearing the news.

'They created a desert and called it peace.' Tacitus.

As a committed Europhobe, Boris now bestrides the political stage like a colossus. His seeming disdain for Europe is only matched by his dismissal of Ireland as some kind of political backwater, unworthy of serious consideration, and Scotland as an ungrateful recipient of Westminster handouts. He's become a serious danger to the Union itself.

The Peloponnese War between Athens and Sparta, two former friends and allies, brought an end to the Golden Age of Classical Greece. With its economy crippled, Athens' democratically elected government was ousted and replaced by the Thirty Tyrants. It was the end of democracy. It never recovered.

The same Boris, who recently referred to the French as 'turds' is hoping to re-negotiate our exit terms when he becomes Prime Minister. Here's a view of him from across the Channel:

JUMP. FATSO!

(from Charlie Hebdo magazine, July 2016)

"I have a face like an elephant's arse" said the great English actor Charles Laughton. Another famous Englishman deserves such an epithet just now: Boris Johnson. Ever since the Brexit vote, his impish, schoolboy features have come to resemble more and more the face of a cartoon coward. When an elephant slopes off, it inevitably shows you its backside and this is pretty much what Boris Johnson has been showing us for a week or more now -a face which looks like an elephant's arse as said pachyderm buggers off, having just trampled all your crops.

Our media circus makes fairground animals out of our political figures. Showbiz beasts who will, to catch the eye of a jaded public, rear on their hind-legs in the middle of the ring with infinitely more alacrity than any weary elephant and commit any contortions to keep the punters happy. Contortions and moral gymnastics were definitely necessary for Boris Johnson to switch from a broadly pro-Europe position to a prominent place amongst the rabid Europhobes. We had thought that Boris Johnson was a politician. But it seems he was merely a circus animal.

For too many politicians, Europe is nothing but a circus. In France, our version of Boris Johnson goes by the name of Nicolas Sarkozy. He, also, is prepared to say almost anything to get the cameras turned in his direction. Boris Johnson spooked the British electorate with nonsensical stunts about the exact shape of bananas permissible under EU regulations. Sarkozy pulls the same spurious legerdemain with similar supposed EU restrictions on the shape of cucumbers. They resemble very much the old notion of 18th century 'wreckers' who would swing lanterns on the coastline during storms to trick mariners into shipwreck upon those coasts, in order to pillage the wrecks for booty. In Jamaica Inn, Charles Laughton plays a country squire and Justice of the Peace who is also the secret leader of the local gang of wreckers. There's something very Boris Johnson about that. The European Union is definitely a kind of big ship.

And often those politicians who should be defending it spend their time trying to shipwreck it – exactly like the upstanding pillar of society played by Laughton in the film – a man expected to uphold the law but who is, in fact, its most implacable enemy.

At the end of Jamaica Inn, Charles Laughton is chased by the mob he has so long swindled and betrayed. He flees to the top of a ship's mast. When he's sure that everyone is looking at him, he throws himself from his refuge and is dashed to pieces on the deck below. Thus, forcing the ugly truth of himself upon the luckless onlookers: the truth that he's nothing but a big fat shit which goes splat when it hits the deck.

So, go on, Fatso, jump! The crowd is waiting. Waiting for Boris and his buddies to do the dignified splatty-type thing. But the crowd will be waiting a long time. Because in the end, Boris Johnson lacks something of Laughton's class. He and the other wreckers of Europe have already scarpered. Look at them disappearing over the horizon.

****

He's tipping the scales now. But is the Writing on the Wall?

Plato, who didn't care much for poets – or democracy either, for that matter; divided the world into two realms. The visible, which we see and grasp; and the intelligible: the mind, or the forms. The former ever changing, the latter, constant. He believed that only the forms could be objects of knowledge because they possessed the unchanging truth of the mind.

Boris must have skimmed over that one in his studies.

It's a different country now: cracks have appeared and the divisions are ever more apparent. Boris and his gang opened the box and emptied its contents. All that remains is Hope.

When the Lake Drops, Neptune Rises

I met Michael Webster at Dove Cottage around twelve years ago. He and poet Paul Farley recorded the nocturnal noises within the house and using a computer program, transcribed the sounds into individual words for their exhibition and installation called 'Amanuensis'. He's the former creative director at Vidal Sassoon and works as a freelance artist and graphic designer. He's aware that I'm constantly in need of new stories and last weekend he took me along to see the strange and largely forgotten 'Inscribed Rocks of Windermere.'

Ecclerigg Crag quarry is an overgrown eighteenth century stone works that lies in the grounds of Crag Wood Country House on the shores of Lake Windermere. The last stone to be extracted built the house in 1910; since then the area has been allowed to self-seed and conceal itself so that these days you wouldn't know it was there until you stumble upon it.

It's the same with the carvings: they appear out of the moss and lichen like riddles: prophetic coded messages and names that you feel must mean something by the extraordinary lengths the mason has gone to in producing them.

We came across the first one in the forest floor, carved into rock that was partially buried and covered in leaf litter and almost two meters in length, it read.

        NATIONAL DEBT L800.000.000   1837
              O, SAVE MY COUNTRY HEAVEN!
              GEORGE 3   WILLIAM PITT
        MONEY IS THE SINEWS OF WAR
       FIELD MARSHALL WELLINGTON
            HEROIC Adm NELSON

Scraping away the moss from the surrounding rocks reveals a litany of names: some bold and incised while others are raised and written in old English.

Wordsworth poet Rydal: Walter Scott Author. Humphrey Davy, Dr Jenner, James Hogg, the explorers Ross and Parry along with less well known figures such as Matthew Piper, a Quaker from Whitehaven whose good deeds in funding and endowing three National schools along with a soup kitchen also gets a mention. Alongside are freedom fighters General Lafayette, Lord Byron and Robin Hood. All are meticulously carved on an industrial scale into the exposed rock. Still others lie below the water line and it's said that when the lake level drops Neptune rises.

The carvings are attributed to a reclusive stonemason called John Longmire from nearby Troutbeck who between 1835 and 1837 took it upon himself to carve the names of his heroes along with other issues of the day onto the exposed rock. Why he did it is unclear; they weren't commissioned as the quarry's absentee owner lived in Devon and rarely if ever set foot on the place. Nor were they done for any kind of public recognition since the area is far from the road or public footpaths. The inclusion of Byron and Lafayette and the omission of the reigning monarch suggest Republican leanings, while Dr Jenner (smallpox vaccine), Davy (the miners' lamp) and to a lesser extent Piper, imply a man with a deep social conscience very much aware of the sufferings of others. Whatever his reasons he's left his mark – though not his name – on the inscribed rocks. A transcript from the Ancient

Monument Society suggests that he was simply 'marking the passage of time through the people and events that had shaped his life.'

It sounds like a good enough reason to me.

Photo of carvings Julie Ellis

Wrecks

"The common people ther do pray for shippes which they sie in danger. They al sit downe upon their knees and hold up their handes and say very devotedly. Lord, send her to us, God send her to us. Seeing them upon their knees, and their hands joined, you do think that they are praying for your sauvette; but their myndes are far from that. They pray, not God to sauve you, or send you to the port, but to send you to them by shipwrack, that they may gette the spoile of her. And to show that this is their meaning, if the shippe come well to porte, or aschew naufrage, they gette up in anger, crying, the Devil stick her, she is away from us."

Robin Rigg, governor of Lindisfarne circa 1643

In the century following the dissolution of the monastery on Lindisfarne, the island community, once a centre of learning and devotion to God, descended into poverty and lawlessness: smuggling was rife and wrecking – the practice of luring ships onto rocks with false lights – had become commonplace, as alluded to by the then governor, Robin Rigg, in conversation with a priest, who had himself narrowly escaped being shipwrecked on the hidden rocks that surround the island while trying to make it to port.

A few miles east of Lindisfarne lie the Farne Islands, an archipelago made up of a dozen or so rocky outposts that are a haven for seals and nesting seabirds. They are also a ships' graveyard having claimed hundreds of vessels and thousands of lives over the centuries. Even with modern navigation equipment and depth finders it's still tricky; and last week my brother Graham, who brought along his charts to plot a navigable route through the rocks and sandbars for his upcoming voyage, joined me on the island.

Graham Ward is the Senior Project Manager for Balfour Engineering. He's based in Newcastle, where he's lived for twenty eight years and much of his work has involved building schools, universities and hospitals around the region: multi-million pound projects that he has to price, tender and build on budget and on time. It's hugely stressful, but meeting him you wouldn't know it as he just takes it all in his stride and gets on with it. Away from work and family, his passion is sailing and he will often take his small boat out into open seas on summer evenings and bracing winter days for the sheer joy and exhilaration of it all.

The wall of the Crown and Anchor pub, where we spent a pleasant evening, carries a chart of Farne island wrecks: it also has an inscription – 'Oh Lord. The sea is so large and my ship, so small.'

A Subterranean World

If from the public way you turn your steps
Up the tumultuous brook of Greenhead Gill.

No habitation there is seen but such
As journey thither find themselves alone
With a few sheep, with rocks and stones, and kites
That overhead are sailing in the sky
It is in truth an utter solitude...

From *Michael* by William Wordsworth

Wordsworth composed his poem in a sheepfold where he sat day after day in quiet contemplation. What he fails to mention in his pastoral idyll was the extensive lead mining that was taking place at the time in the foothills of the mountain beside the beck. A number of these tunnels, now overgrown and flooded, remain, and the other weekend I went along with Andy Astle to explore an early Elizabethan settlement and mine on the rocky slopes.

Andy's family moved to Grasmere from Morecambe when he was thirteen to run a guesthouse in the village. He began his working life as the village postman before moving into management and he now runs the regional delivery centre in Barrow. He enjoys cycling and walking and when he offered to take me down one of the disused mines of Greenhead Ghyll he'd explored many years ago – it was an opportunity I couldn't pass up.

Lead is formed by heat and pressure when sub-vertical mineral veins merge with hot fluids in the earth to form seams. Bluish white when extracted it oxidises when exposed to air turning it silver / grey. Its low melting temperature, requiring little more than a campfire, made it one of the earliest metals to be exploited and it's been in use for around 8000 years.

In 1564 a group of German miners (valued for their expertise) built a settlement alongside the beck and for the next nine years burrowed deep into the mountain. It was abandoned in 1573 and since that time nature has done its best to reclaim the land, where these days only a scattering of rough-cut stones and broken walls, and a partially concealed and flooded tunnel remain.

The entrance isn't much wider than a man and I followed Andy feet first into icy water that sent a shock wave through me after the heat of the day and the steep ascent. It was just big enough to stand up in; with the water up to our chests, and using the walls to steady ourselves we made our way inside the mountain.

The tunnel runs for around four hundred feet: its rough walls shaped by picks and gunpowder formed an arc just above our heads. I found myself in awe of the courage and tenacity of the men who worked and possibly died here four hundred and fifty years ago. I continued in for about fifty feet until a slip on the uneven floor almost put the camera in the water, and while enjoying the moment, I had no particular desire to have to repeat the experience with another camera. I let Andy go on ahead while I took some pictures, then turned away from the black subterranean world and made my way out; emerging into the bright, beautiful day.

Even the Cows Love it

Each generation makes the landscape its own. We are all of us simply temporary managers of the places we inherit or buy – it's all ephemeral.

For years now, farmers have been having a hard time. Victims of supermarket price wars and government legislation they've been forced to adapt and diversify in the way that few other industries have. So vitally important and yet so easily overlooked and taken for granted.

Eric and Amanda Dowson are third generation Ribble Valley dairy farmers who tend a couple of hundred acres a few miles north of Blackburn. I did my apprenticeship there in the late seventies and continued to work there periodically over twenty-five years. At one time their pedigree herd supplied most of east Lancashire with milk and cream, but these days it goes in to making their award winning ice cream. Even the cows love it, and while I don't really have a sweet tooth and am obviously somewhat biased I feel I can say with some certainty that it's the finest ice cream you'll taste.

They have no issue with sharing their land with native wildlife; as Eric says: 'they also need somewhere to live and the land is as much theirs as it is his.' They are a truly progressive farming family who I'm happy to write about and endorse.

It could have been so different. In 2001 when Foot and Mouth blighted the northern counties they were in serious danger of losing their herd, and it was only through a monumental effort involving thousands of gallons of disinfectant and the strictest of procedures for those entering and leaving the farm, that kept the disease away.

With the herd still intact they began to diversify. We planted up a six-acre field with maize: Eric drew a witch on a draughtboard to scale. We then marked out a grid in the field and when the corn was at waist height, with Eric holding the map and directing, I cut a giant maze in the shape of a witch in the shadow of Pendle Hill. From its humble beginnings it's now expanded into Scare Kingdom and attracts thousands of visitors a year. They also began to make their own ice cream and opened a café and animal park. The ice cream business continues to grow. They make a ton and a half a week and there's always a surplus that most manufacturers would reprocess, but they see it as a waste product and give it back to the cows instead. They love it and have come to regard it as a midweek treat.

The spectacle of cows eating ice cream was one I shan't forget.

Of Sorcery

It was on a Lammas night,
When corn rigs are bonie,
Beneath the moon's unclouded light,
I held away to Annie:
The time flew by, wi tentless heed,
Till 'tween the late and early;
Wi' sma' persuasion she agreed
To see me thro' the barley.

From *The Rigs O' Barley* by Robert Burns

Lammas Night was one of the four major pagan festivals. It took place on the 1st of August and celebrated the harvesting of cereal crops and summer fruits. Fresh loaves would be baked and placed in circles, and later, churches as an offering of thanksgiving. The festival also commemorated the end of summer and the waning days of autumn.

I mention all this now as I've just returned with Jodie and Hung from Long Meg and her Daughters, a late Neolithic stone circle east of Penrith; where the remains of such votive offerings were still visible among the stones.

Jodie Phillips and Hung-Chun Huang studied Mexican and Chinese literature at Newcastle and Kaohsiung universities (Taiwan) respectively, while Hung completed an MA in English literature at Lancaster. Like Kat and Susan (see 'The Italian Job'), they work as trainees at the Wordsworth Trust. Professionally and socially they are great friends and are a delight and an inspiration to work alongside. One evening after work we took a drive out to the stone circle.

Of the thirteen hundred or so circles around the British Isle Long Meg is one of the largest. Meg herself stands over ten feet high and is a nine-ton block of red sandstone that was originally brought up from the riverbed two miles away. It bears cup and ring markings and is positioned to align with the mid-winter sun. The Daughters are made from granite: around seventy in total, they form a ring beside her. There are numerous legends associated with the stones the most famous being that of sorcery and petrification. A Scottish wizard called Michael Scott, while passing through the area, came across a coven of witches and turned them into stone. It is said that the stones cannot be counted and that whoever manages to reach the same number twice, will break the spell and release them.

Just for the record we managed sixty-four, sixty-seven and sixty-nine.

The Problem with Africa

Donald Trump on Africa:

'We are having all these people from shithole countries come here!'

And in a tweet aimed at Somalia-born Democrat, Ilhan Omar:

'Why don't they go back and help fix the totally broken and crime infested places from which they came. Whose governments are a complete catastrophe, the worst, most corrupt and inept anywhere in the world?'

Nigel Farage:

'Women could be at risk of sex attacks carried out by gangs of migrant men.'

Boris Johnson:

'Sirte [Libya] could be the next Dubai, once they clear away the dead bodies'

With these remarks the perception and portrayal of Africa and Africans as savage, corrupt and uncivilized continues. And while there is no denying the conflicts and massacres that have occurred in recent times: Biafra, Rwanda, Mozambique, Sudan, Sierra

Leone, Congo… At the same time, it's important to understand the root causes.

The photograph was taken by Alice Seeley Harris, a missionary in the Belgian Congo in the early twentieth century. It's a picture of Nsala, staring at the severed hand and foot of his five-year-old daughter, Boali.

In 1885 the Belgian King Leopold, claimed 240.000 square kilometres either side of the Congo River as his 'own personal slice of the African cake.' He claimed to be on a philanthropic mission to end slavery and civilize the region. In reality he intended to get very rich off the high demand for rubber from the trees that grew naturally there. To achieve this, he formed a rubber company with its own private army. Armed militia would enter villages, hold the women and children hostage, sending out the men to find and tap rubber trees. They were given quotas, failure to meet them resulted in death or mutilation.

Alice Seeley Harris encountered Nsala in the aftermath of one such raid. She would later recount the story in her book, *Don't Call Me Lady*.

He hadn't made his rubber quota for the day so the Belgian-appointed overseers had cut off his daughter's hand and foot. Her name was Boali. She was five years old. Then they killed her. But they weren't finished. Then they killed his wife too. And because that didn't seem quite cruel enough, quite strong enough to make their case, they cannibalized both Boali and her mother. And they presented Nsala with the tokens, the leftovers from the once living body of his darling child whom he so loved. His life was destroyed. They had partially destroyed it anyway by forcing his servitude but this act finished it for him.

All of this filth had occurred because one man, one man who lived thousands of miles across the sea, one man who couldn't get rich enough, had decreed that this land was his and that these people should serve his own greed.

Leopold's quest for rubber: the *'Unimaginable horror'* as Conrad had it, resulted in the deaths of up to 10 million people.

Forty years earlier, while travelling through East Africa in search of the source of the Nile, the explorers Sir Richard Burton and John Hanning Speke encountered first-hand the then thousand-year-old Arab slave trade. Burton was a well-travelled, worldly man, but the horrors they witnessed would haunt Burton for the rest of his life.

He recalls one such incident involving their Arab guide.

The Kirangozi or Mnyamwezi guide, who had accompanied the Expedition from the coast, remained behind, because his newly-purchased slave-girl had become foot-sore, and unable to advance; finding the case hopeless, he cut off her head, lest of his evil good might come to another.

Africa has been traumatized. And having endured so much suffering it should come as no surprise that the African countries – the map of the continent, created by foreign powers – should have struggled to stabilise and democratise in the post-colonial era. The demarcation lines between countries, rather than running along natural boundaries such as rivers and mountains, are drawn in a grid-like system, cutting through traditional tribal borders. It has the effect of empowering one group whilst dividing and weakening another. Massacres in Biafra and Rwanda were a direct result of this.

It's equally unsurprising that brutal dictators such as Amin and Mobuto should emerge from the colonial wreckage. The likelihood of an abused child becoming an abuser themselves is proportionally high. Power, they've witnessed, is maintained through intimidation and fear.

That much of Africa has managed to come to terms with its past and overcome these difficulties, emerging as peaceful law-abiding democracies with small, but vibrant economies, is something to admire and applaud. But there's still some way to go,

All of which brings us to the present, where a new geo-political push for Africa is taking place. China, Russia and now the US, are all moving in for a slice of the cake. If history teaches us anything, you can guarantee that the interests and welfare of the African people won't be the priority. What Africa needs is investment in transport and infrastructure which would allow the smaller countries to trade with each other. The resources are there, it just needs the logistics and political will and vision to carry it through. A continent-wide trade-bloc would be beneficial to all.

These are new countries taking first steps. The brutality and barbarism of the not-so-distant past sit uneasily beneath the surface. In many places power still resides in the barrel of a gun and people continue to be forced from their homes and land. The current migrant crisis, seized upon by populist politicians for political gain, is a direct result of this. But, when they pause and ask themselves, *why* these countries can't stabilise, and why the conflicts and arbitrary massacres seem almost cyclical, I would suggest they look at the photo of Nsala with the remains of his daughter – his punishment for not collecting enough rubber – and find their answers there.

Taking it for Granted

You'd have thought that freedom of choice and expression along with access to information, were not just a right, but a basic necessity. Like eating and breathing they are the things that allow us to think and function within society. We take it for granted and rightly so, because few people who were born in this country and are alive today will have known any different. Yet it's less than a hundred years ago that women were given the right to vote; and up until relatively recent times the opportunities for upward social mobility were very much dependent on where you lived and which school you attended.

Paul Hebson is a former footballer who played for the County and later coached the Grasmere football team. He's the secretary of the Reading Rooms, a social club, which plays an important role as an alternative space for local people, where for a small annual subscription members can get together to play games and socialize away from the bustling hubbub of seasonal visitors.

Formerly a Workman's Reading Room it was founded by a local woman, Elisabeth Agger, in the mid-nineteenth century, as a place where quarrymen and farm workers might retire after a hard day's work to read books, newspapers and periodicals; and while it's no longer used as a reading room per se, a selection of books from the period are displayed in a cabinet inside. Paul and a small committee run the club, and in a village where most property is unaffordable to local people, it's reassuring to know it can never be sold.

In the eighteenth and early nineteenth centuries libraries operated by subscription and newspapers were heavily taxed, which limited circulation to a few thousand units and had the effect of keeping the readership selective. In the aftermath of the French Revolution the authorities were fearful of a similar situation developing here and it was felt by many in government that educating the working classes above basic literacy levels could radicalise them; disrupting the 'natural order' leading to social unrest and revolution. The same irrational argument was still being mooted decades later when benefactors like Elizabeth Agger built and endowed reading rooms in towns and villages up and down the country. They were social reformers; individuals who put their own money and reputations on the line for the common good, and in doing so played a significant role in making books, news and information available to all.

We do take it for granted, but at the same time it's also worth remembering that it hasn't always been like this.

Below is an excerpt from Shelley's poem The Masque of Anarchy, written in response to the Peterloo massacre of 1819 and described by his publisher Leigh Hunt as a flaming robe of verse; its publication was suppressed and it didn't appear in print until 1832, ten years after the poet's death.

What is Freedom? Ye can tell
That which Slavery is too well,
For its very name has grown
To an echo of your own.

Let a vast assembly be,
And with great solemnity
Declare with measured words, that ye
Are, as God has made ye, free.

The old laws of England—they
Whose reverend heads with age are grey,
Children of a wiser day;

*And whose solemn voice must be
Thine own echo—Liberty!*

*Rise, like lions after slumber
In unvanquishable number!
Shake your chains to earth like dew
Which in sleep had fallen on you:
Ye are many—they are few!"*

Percy Bysshe Shelley

Austerity Chicken with Colin Marshall

These are austere times for many families. The 'tightening of belts' is squeezing the life out of many of our communities. Minimum wage jobs, zero hours and short-term contracts, flexi-hours; coupled with welfare cuts which has reduced government borrowing while at the same time increasing household debt for poorer families. A million people regularly use food banks and the gulf between the haves and have-nots is increasing at an alarming rate.

Sound familiar? If this applies to you help is at hand (providing you like chicken). Musician and chef Colin Marshall, using one large chicken and some assorted veg, created thirteen dinners, enough to feed two people for nearly a week at a total cost of fifteen quid.

Colin hails from Southport shrimping stock. He left school at sixteen to work in a sheet metal factory and later attended university where he read History and Politics, before going on to complete a post-grad at Bristol in Vocational Studies. He became a careers advisor before dropping out himself and living in a squat in Amsterdam for two years. He fell into chefing in his mid-thirties, but music is his real passion and when not working in the kitchen he's playing and teaching guitar in the area.

He has a deep social conscience and the other week he set himself a challenge to create a week's worth of nutritious meals for the price of a takeaway. I went along afterwards to interview him.

The audio recording of this interview can be found on the My Backyard blog:

www.markwardpoet.co.uk/backyard/austerity-chicken-with-colin-marshall/

Michael and the Great Feast

Michael Mitchell studied history at Southampton University, before moving to Grasmere in 1993, where he helps manage the Wordsworth gift shop and works in finance. His interests are vernacular architecture, classic rail journeys and social history. Never a slave to fashion he wears his Marillion t-shirts with pride – he's also a friend to many and the other week to celebrate his 20th anniversary we held a great feast in the orchard in his honour.

Of all the social and political changes that have occurred in my lifetime, the T.V dinner probably did more damage to family and social cohesion than any wider governmental policies. My generation left the dining table for the couch and with it the daily ritual of sharing a meal and a conversation. Glued to the telly with our meals on our laps we'd eat our evening meals in virtual silence. It suited us at the time but it isn't something I'd personally advocate now, as there's nothing quite like a communal meal for bringing people together.

The Wordsworth Trust employs around fifty people in varying capacities and many of us reside in the hamlet of Town End at the edge of Grasmere village. We live and work together and it's the first time since I was a kid that I've lived in a community where everyone knows and looks out for each other. When we decided to throw a feast in honour of one of our longest and most popular residents a good attendance was virtually guaranteed.

We arranged it in the Old English style with benches and a great banqueting table: we had a bonfire, minstrels and – a modern touch – a rack of throwaway barbecues. I'd have liked to have included some archery or perhaps some displays of swordsmanship but we had to draw the line somewhere…

When the sun went down we lit lanterns and when the music stopped the crackling fire and mellifluous flow of conversation filled the night. It was the most magical of evenings.

We could do a lot worse than have a national day of feasting, similar to Thanksgiving where communities come together to share a meal. In the meantime I'm looking forward to Michael's 40th.

Seeking out the Thin Places

Anyone visiting or living in the Lake District, or any other place of natural beauty for that matter; and who are sensitive and at peace within themselves and their environment will have on occasion sat on a rock, a bench, a tussock; looked out across a valley and in a period of quiet reflection absorbed that scene into their subconscious. It remains there to be revisited at quiet moments by your desk, at home or in the city, when the treadmill of daily life begins to grind at your spirit and sanity, inducing an inner peace: a sanctuary.

In his book *Walking into Celtic Spirituality* Cameron Butland refers to these areas of natural beauty as Thin Places: where the separation between heaven and earth, the physical and the spiritual is almost imperceptible; and where the early Celtic Christians of the first millennium through solitude, prayer and meditation sought the Creator in his creation. Some of the places he mentions such as Iona, Lindisfarne and St David's are well known – others more obscure. St Bega's chapel on the shores of Lake Bassenthwaite is one such place and last week, on a rare sunny day I went along with Cameron to visit the historic site.

Cameron studied archaeology at the University of East Anglia before training for the ministry at Ripon College, Oxford. He was ordained at Lichfield Cathedral in 1984 and since then has served in the dioceses of Lichfield, Oxford and Carlisle. He is currently the rector of St Oswald's, Grasmere. He has a Masters in historical research; teaches church history and leads regular quiet days and courses on Celtic spirituality, prayer and psychology.

We took the footpath from Dodd Wood car park skirting Mire House and made our way through the outbuildings and woodland until we reached the edge of the estate where the valley opened out before us. Cameron stopped and sweeping his arm before him said 'Look, this is what I mean.' It was breathtakingly beautiful. In the bright sunlight the stream cut through the soft emerald pasture like hot metal turning the lake platinum, while the port wine stains of blushing heather against the grey rock of the high surrounding fells combined to form a palette that was as rich as it was sublime. He went on, 'When you see this you can't help being affected by its beauty and majesty: the feeling runs deep, bringing you closer to nature and in the Celtic Christian tradition, to God.'

Cameron was a learned and erudite companion; along the way we discussed the poetry of Caedmon and Blake; Armitage and Duffy. He spoke of the symbolism of water to pray in or beside, and the social impact of the Norman invasion and the establishing of the Roman church with its warring popes and political agendas, replacing a church that had been more communal and spiritually grounded in the natural world. He talked of the hermit Anthony of Egypt; and how the early pioneers of the church in this country followed his example by living a life of solitude and prayer in remote parts of the British Isles.

St Bega was one such pioneer. She is believed to have been an Irish princess, who sailed to England in the seventh century and formed a religious community at St Bega's Bay, now St Bees. At some point she chose to leave her community behind and travelled inland to the shores of Lake Bassenthwaite, where she lived out her life as a hermit. The site later became a place of pilgrimage and in the thirteenth century a Norman chapel was built where her dwelling had once stood. A pilgrims cross stands at the entrance: Cameron mounted the steps and kneeling kissed the base of the cross as pilgrims would have done in times past; giving thanks for a safe deliverance.

A mile from the nearest road and accessible only on foot it is still a place of peace and tranquillity and we lingered a while before making our way back along the well-trodden path to our starting point.

The Song of Caedmon

Now let me praise the keeper of Heavens kingdom,
The might of the Creator and his thought,
The work of the Father of glory, how each of wonders
The Eternal Lord established in the beginning.
He first created for the sons of men
Heaven as a roof, the holy Creator,
Then middle-earth the keeper of mankind,
The Eternal Lord, afterwards made,
The earth for men, the Almighty Lord.

Paradise Lane

In the parable of the Good Samaritan, a Jewish traveller is stripped, beaten and left for dead at the side of the road. A priest and Levite come along and seeing him, cross to the opposite side of the road and pass by. Later, a Samaritan, a traditional enemy of the Jews, comes by and seeing him takes pity. He bathes and binds his wounds, gives him his own cloak, places him on his donkey and takes him to an inn where he cares for him at his own expense.

Variations on the theme are to be found in all the major religions, where charity and compassion towards those who are suffering is rightly upheld to be one of our great human virtues.

With this in mind it should therefore come as a surprise to learn that of the 1,237 towns and cities within the UK, less than twenty percent of those accept refugees and asylum seekers. Our great virtue has been politicised and despite the fact that refugees account for less than five percent of total migration into this country annually, they take up a disproportionate amount of negative publicity in the national press. My hometown of Blackburn takes in refugees and in order to better understand what is ultimately, a worldwide crisis, I've been spending time at the ARC Asylum and Refugee Centre on Paradise Lane. It's been an enlightening experience.

There are twenty-five million refugees globally. People fleeing war, persecution, famine and poverty and each year a tiny proportion of those make their way to our shores. Having introduced myself to the group, I pinned a world map to the wall and using a felt pen asked them to mark their journeys. From Central America and China, through Africa and the Middle and Far East, the lines began to resemble a cat's cradle crisscrossing the world.

Among them, an Afghan woman who escaped with her two young daughters after the Taliban came to the house and took away her eldest daughter, forcing her into marriage. Another Afghan woman trekked through the mountains with her family for fifteen days. When they got to the shores of the Aegean, they handed over what little money they had and put to sea at night in a rubber dinghy with over forty other passengers. During the night a boat pulled alongside and slashed the dinghy, sinking it. Most drowned; she and her family managed to stay afloat and were eventually picked up by a Greek patrol boat. I met a civil engineer from Syria who escaped through the mountains with his family when Isis attacked their town; an albino man from Africa whose seven-month journey took him through the jungle and Sahara Desert; a young family from El Salvador escaping violence; an old woman from the Congo, formerly Zaire, who remembered listening to Muhammed Ali's Rumble in the Jungle on the communal radio in her village. One man pointed to the Mediterranean and said simply, "Graveyard." So many epic journeys, so many stories, so much suffering. Most I spoke with hadn't come here for a better life; they'd come here that they might live.

At the Centre, Sister Marie teaches English grammar, volunteers serve tea and toast while Syd and her assistants help with navigating the labyrinthine maze of paperwork: applications, rejections and appeals: the false summits of hope. A shuffling paper trail wending its way through our ponderous bureaucracy.

They are a mixed group of men, women and children of all ages. Some are embroidering a tapestry to present to the UN, with each stitch representing a refugee. They feel safe here. The town's multi-ethnic population allows them to live quietly and begin rebuilding their lives. One Iranian man, a former political prisoner, questioned why anyone would want to live in London when they could live in Darwen. "Darwen" he declared "is beautiful."

When refugee status is approved it automatically extends to their family. In poorer countries where resources are limited a family will select the strongest and fittest of the group, often a young male and pool their money, before sending him on the long arduous journey in the hope he'll get through and help get them out. Very few, I learned, were single men as such.

And then I'm looking at the map of Europe and remembering back to the time when we were the EUs economic migrants. When unemployment hit three million in the early 80s, thousands of us took advantage of our Common Market membership and went to work on German building sites, in French vineyards, Dutch factories and Greek hostels and tavernas. Along with providing employment when there wasn't any here, it opened our eyes to the world.

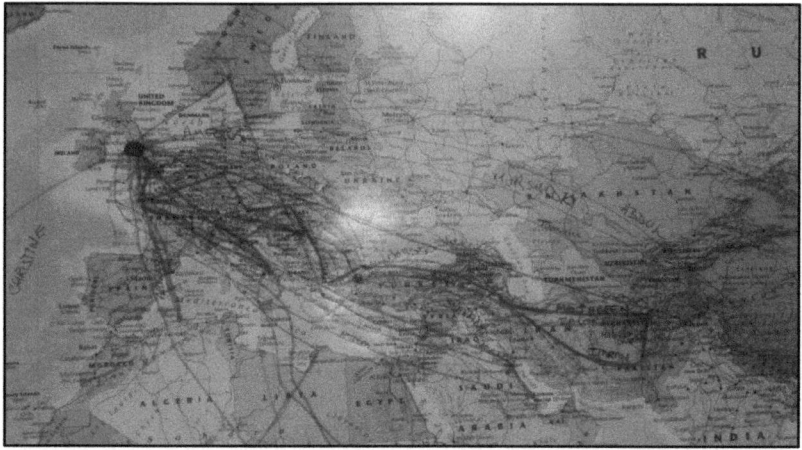

The map is making me restless and I find myself tracing my own journey. Through Deck Access and the Lodestar, past Green Lane and Mellor Brook: across the Irish Sea. I'm moving through Canada and Alaska, Australia and New Zealand, Malaysia, the Himalayas, the Middle East and Africa.

The countless paths, the twists and turns; the trajectory of a life that took me around the world before placing me here: a kindred spirit among fellow wanderers, at the ARC Refugee Centre, in the Methodist Mission on Paradise Lane.

RECIPES

Leo's recipe for Sloe Gin	**110**
Dorothy Wordsworth's recipe for Boiled Gooseberry Jam	**110**
Donald's recipe for Steak and Kidney Pudding	**110**
Annalie's recipe for Easy Scottish Flapjacks	**111**
Ian's 'Yammed' Stew	**112**
Stewart's recipe for Quiche	**112**
Catherine's recipe for Fish Pie	**113**
Rick's recipe for Faeryland Hot Pink Mulled Apple Juice	**114**
Sally's recipe for Walnut and Cinnamon Scones	**115**
David's recipe for Jamaican Jerked Chicken	**115**
Malie's Recipe for Sticky Toffee Pudding	**116**
Tony and Mo's recipe for Peasant Soup	**117**
Jules's Prize Winning Burgers	**118**
Esther's recipe for Morecambe Potted Shrimps	**119**
Mark's recipe for Farmers' Fingers	**119**
Susan and Kat's recipe for *A Little Bowl of Sunshine*	**120**
Alex's recipe for Chocolate Stout Cake	**121**
Dean's recipe for *Townend Ruby Murray Without the Hurry*	**122**
Michael's recipe for Marbled Eggs	**124**
Andy's recipe for Alternative Gingerbread	**125**
Amanda's recipe for a Simple Dish of Mushroom Soup with a Hunk of Warm Bread and Butter	**126**
Hung's recipe for *Coffin Lid*	**127**
Colin's Leftover Chicken Pasties	**128**
Mrs Mitchell's Dorset Apple Cake	**129**

Leo's recipe for Sloe Gin

Requirements
1 large preserving jar
Enough sloes to fill jar
Granulated sugar
Bottle of gin

Fill jar with frozen sloes
Pour in sugar tapping jar to make sure it fills all cavities
Fill jar to the top with gin: seal and leave for a minimum of three months, shaking jar gently every now and then. The longer left the better.

Dorothy Wordsworth's recipe for Boiled Gooseberry Jam
7th August 1800

Boiled gooseberries – NB 2lbs of sugar in the first panful, 3 quarts all good measure – 3lb in the 2nd 4 quarts – 2 ½ lb in the 3rd

Donald's recipe for Steak and Kidney Pudding
Ingredients:
Three pounds (value) diced steak and kidney
One large onion
One oxo cube
Black pudding
Mushrooms
One egg

Short crust pastry

Place steak and kidney in a pan and bring to the boil: add chopped onion and black pudding: sprinkle oxo cube then leave to simmer for two hours adding mushrooms (optional) later on.

When the meat is tender place an eggcup at the centre of your baking dish and carefully pour out the contents making sure to wiggle the eggcup so that you don't get an air-lock. (It could blow the lid off!) Roll out the pastry and place it over the dish – the eggcup will prevent it collapsing – seal and brush with a beaten egg and place in the oven for thirty-five minutes.

I haven't tried it yet but it sounds delicious.

Annalie's recipe for Easy Scottish Flapjacks

Put 6oz butter, 6oz soft brown sugar and 3 tablespoons of golden syrup in a pan and heat gently. When the butter has melted, remove from the heat and stir in 8oz porridge oats (you can stir in some chocolate chips as well if you like).

Turn mixture into a greased tin and bake for 15 minutes at 180c or gas mark 4 (don't overcook it; flapjack should be soft and chewy). Leave to cool, then cut into squares.

If taking on a picnic, wrap in foil. Beware of ticks when eating out and about; they won't attack your flapjack, but they *will* attack you.

Note:

If you don't have any weighing scales, use about ¾ packet butter, a cup of sugar and 3 cups of oats.

Ian's recipe for `Yammed' Stew

Ingredients:

Stewing beef or mince, potatoes, carrots, swede, white cabbage, broth mix, mushrooms, bay leaf, Worcester sauce, stock cubes and gravy granules.

Method:

Put one cup of broth mix in a large pan and bring to the boil, then simmer for half an hour. Prepare the vegetables and when broth mix is ready add one large bay leaf, a dash of Worcester sauce, salt and pepper to taste and any herbs you may fancy. Add stock cubes to taste and the meat and vegetables. Use gravy granules to thicken the mixture to your liking: top up with water to cover all then bring to boil and let it bubble away gently for about twenty minutes, stirring occasionally until you're satisfied that it is done.

Any of the vegetables may be left out if desired.

Git yokked inti'l it.

Stewart's recipe for Quiche

Ingredients:

Short crust pastry (make or buy)

Three eggs

Milk (third of a pint)

One onion

Stick of celery

Teaspoon of mustard

Grated cheese

Salt and pepper

Sweetcorn and 'whatever else you've got lying around in the fridge'

Roll out pastry into tray, press into the sides: trim off the surplus and place in the oven at 200C and bake until it smells nice. Fry celery and onions until soft: beat eggs and milk adding mustard, salt and pepper along with other ingredients and stir evenly. Place in the oven and bake until it sets. Serve with a baked potato.

Catherine's recipe for Fish Pie

Ingredients

250ml fish stock

250ml milk (plus a bit to put in the mashed potatoes)

350g assorted fish

1 bay leaf

750g mashed potatoes

50g butter

1 leek – washed and sliced

50g plain flour

1tbsp fresh parsley

Salt and pepper

A generous handful of grated cheese

Method

Heat the oven to 180^0 C, gas mark 4.

Pour the fish stock and milk into a large saucepan and bring to a simmer.

Add the fish, which should be in bite size chunks – use either all one sort of fish, or a mixture (I always add a few prawns too) of fleshy, non-oily fish like salmon or cod.

Add the bay leaf and poach for 5 minutes.

Remove the fish and put to one side; don't throw the poaching liquid away as you will be using it later.

Melt the butter in a saucepan over a medium heat. Add the sliced leek and cook for 5 minutes until the leek is soft.

Add the flour and stir well, then pour in the poaching liquid and stir again; turn the heat up and cook for about 3 minutes until the sauce has slightly thickened. Turn the heat off; remove the bay leaf, then add the fish, chopped parsley and some salt and pepper.

Put the mixture into an ovenproof dish and leave to cool slightly.

Cover the fish mixture with a thick layer of mashed potatoes – make sure your fish mixture is not too hot when you do this, otherwise the potato will sink. The resulting mush will be edible, but won't look it.

Sprinkle grated cheese over the top.

Put the dish onto a baking tray (in case it bubbles over during cooking) and bake for 20-30 minutes (until the sauce is bubbling under the potatoes)

Serve with vegetables of your choice – I favour frozen peas, and would advise against cauliflower on aesthetic grounds.

This recipe should feed 4 people.

Rick's recipe for Faeryland Hot Pink Mulled Apple Juice – looks fantastic, smells wonderful, tastes great and is good for you.

Make a bouquet garni consisting of Saigon cinnamon, cloves, ginger, lemon, lime, sencha green tea and Sudanese organic hibiscus (ready made packs available from Faeryland). Add to 1/2 litre of just boiled water. Leave it to infuse for 20 minutes or until the water has turned deep pink.
Add 1 litre of pure apple juice and place in the fridge. Heat to serve.
You may wish to add a sneaky red wine or sloe gin to the heated drink for that extra kick.

Sally's recipe for Walnut and Cinnamon Scones

1lb flour
2 teaspoons of baking powder
2oz of butter
1 tablespoon sugar
2 tablespoons chopped walnuts
1 egg
1 teaspoon ground cinnamon
Milk to mix
Pinch of salt

Make a light scone mixture. Roll out quickly. Sprinkle cinnamon, sugar and nuts over it. Fold in three, then roll to required thickness: cut into shapes and bake in a hot oven on an un-greased baking tray for about ten minutes, or until done.
Delicious spread with rum butter.

David's recipe for Jamaican Jerked Chicken
Ingredients
5 pounds chicken pieces
2 cups distilled white vinegar, plus 1 tsp
2 cups finely chopped scallions
2 Scotch Bonnets, seeded and minced (please wear gloves)
2 tbsps soy sauce
4 tbsps fresh lime juice
5 tsps ground allspice
2 bay leaves
6 cloves garlic, minced
1 tbsp salt

2 tsps sugar

1 ½ tsps dried thyme, crumbled

1 tsp cinnamon

2 cups Jamaican Barbecue sauce, to serve

Directions

Rinse chicken pieces well in 2 cups of the vinegar, drain, transfer to 2 sealable plastic bags and set aside.

In the bowl of a food processor combine remaining 1 tsp vinegar, scallions, Scotch Bonnets, soy sauce, lime juice, allspice, bay leaves, garlic, salt, sugar, thyme, and cinnamon. Reserve 2 tbsps of this marinade for the Jamaican Barbecue Sauce.

Rinse chicken pieces well under cold running water and pat dry with paper towel. Divide chicken pieces between 2 heavy-duty gallon plastic sealable bags and divide marinade evenly between the two. Turn bags over to evenly distribute marinade, and refrigerate the chicken for at least 24 hours and up to 2 days.

On an oiled grill rack set about 6 inches above red-hot coals, grill chicken (in batches if necessary), covered, for 10 to 15 minutes on each side, or until cooked through. Transfer to a warm platter and keep warm until serving.

Serve with Jamaican Barbecue Sauce, alongside fried plantains, rice, or bread of choice.

Malie's Recipe for Sticky Toffee Pudding

4 oz soft butter

6 oz caster sugar

3 beaten eggs

8 oz self-raising flour

8 oz stoned dates, chopped and covered with ½ pint boiling water and left to stand

1 tsp bicarb of soda

1tsp vanilla extract

1 tbsp camp coffee

large handful of sultanas

Mix bicarb of soda, vanilla extract, camp coffee together and add in the handful of sultanas – put to one side

Cream the butter and sugar, then slowly add the beaten egg and fold in the flour. Pour in the vanilla / coffee mixture, add the dates and mix everything together (the consistency should be runny). Turn into an eight-inch cake tin and bake for 1 ½ hours at gas mark 4.

For the sauce

3 oz brown sugar

2 oz butter

3 tbsp double cream

Heat gently until the sugar has dissolved and pour over the finished pudding. Serve with vanilla ice-cream (delicious).

Tony and Mo's recipe for Peasant Soup

1 oz butter
1 lb stewing steak, cut into ¾in. – 1in. cubes
1 medium onion, roughly chopped
Bouquet garni
1 garlic clove, crushed
1 tsp. paprika
Salt & pepper to taste
2 tbsp. plain flour
2 pts good beef stock
1 large potato
Caraway seeds & grated parmesan to garnish

Melt butter until foam subsides and fry the cubes of beef until well browned.

Add the onions, reduce the heat and cook until soft and transparent.

Add the bouquet garni, garlic, paprika salt and pepper and stir well.

Mix in the flour, reduce the heat and cook stirring for 5 mins.

Gradually stir in the stock bringing to the boil, cover the pan and simmer
for 2 hrs.

Add the diced potato, cover the pan and simmer for a further 45mins.

Remove the bouquet garni, and ladle (piping hot) into warmed soup bowls.

Scatter with caraway seeds and grated parmesan if desired but definitely recommended!

PS Depending on appetite, this makes roughly 4 portions and freezes well.

Jules's Prize Winning Burgers

800g minced steak
1 egg
3 slices of sandwich bread, without crust, diced and mixed in a splash of worcester sauce, HP brown sauce, tabasco sauce
1 tbsp tomato puree
1 tsp of Coleman's English Mustard
1 tsp garlic salt
1 tsp celery salt
pepper

All mixed together cold, cover up and refrigerate for two or three hours, divide into four patties.

Esther's recipe for Morecambe Bay Potted Shrimp

Here's the recipe for Morecambe Bay Potted Shrimps, which have been enjoyed as a local delicacy since at least the 18th century:

Ingredients
¼ pack of butter
Good pinch of ground nutmeg
1 pint picked shrimps (ideally from Morecambe Bay)
Salt and pepper

Place the butter in a pan to melt with the pepper and a good pinch of nutmeg.
Once melted, add the shrimps. Stir well over the heat and season – you won't need much salt as the shrimps are already quite salty!
Place the shrimps into little pots or tea cups (1 per person) and press down.
Top with the remaining butter left in the bottom of the pan and chill in the fridge, or can be served warm straight away.
Perfect on hot brown toast or with a watercress salad.

Mark's recipe for Farmers' Fingers

Ingredients

Chicken goujons

Streaky bacon

Dark soy sauce

1 red pepper

1 onion

Broccoli

Savoy cabbage

1 leek

Mixed herbs

Potatoes

Gravy granules

Method

Boil potatoes with chopped leek and cabbage, then drain and mash together with butter.

While the spuds are boiling wrap the chicken in streaky bacon: sprinkle with herbs and shallow fry until chicken turns golden, then add a good lashing of soy sauce.

Add chopped onion, pepper and broccoli: stir and simmer until cooked.

Make up a thick gravy and indulge yourself.

Susan and Kat's recipe for A Little Bowl of Sunshine (aka Veggie Chilli)

Salt, pepper and any other herbs and spices you want to use (e.g. oregano, thyme, cumin, paprika, chilli powder)
Onion
Couple of carrots
Pepper, any colour
Sweet potato
Can of chopped tomatoes
Can of lentils
Can of red kidney beans
Chocolate (preferably dark)

Peel and chop the sweet potato, spread out onto a baking tray with olive oil and whatever herbs and spices you are using. Pop into an oven at 180°C for about ½ hour or so.
Meanwhile, chop the onion, carrots and pepper.
Start frying the onion first with oil, herbs and spices. Then throw the carrots in, then the pepper.
Mix in the chopped tomatoes and let it bubble away for as long as you like. Throw in some chocolate, taste and keep adding chocolate until you reach your desired level of chocolatey-ness.
At the end, mix in the lentils and the beans. Take the sweet potato out of the oven and mix that in too.
Enjoy!

Alex's recipe for Chocolate Stout Cake

Ingredients

Serves 12-14

250ml (9fl oz) Stout (we recommend Coniston Special Oatmeal Stout) and a pint for the chef

250g (9oz) unsalted butter

80g (3oz) cocoa powder

400g (14oz) caster sugar

2 eggs

1 tsp vanilla essence

140ml (5fl oz) buttermilk

280g (10oz) plain flour

2 tsp bicarbonate of soda

½ tsp baking powder

50g (1¾oz) unsalted butter, softened

300g (10½oz) icing sugar

125g (4½oz) full-fat cream cheese (such as Philadelphia)

Cocoa powder, for dusting (optional)

one 23cm (9in) diameter spring-form cake tin

Method

1. Preheat the oven to 170°C (325°F)/gas mark 3, then line the base of the tin with baking parchment.

2. Pour the stout into a saucepan, add the butter and gently heat until it has melted. Remove the pan from the heat and stir the cocoa powder and sugar into the warm liquid. Mix together the eggs, vanilla essence and buttermilk by hand in a jug or bowl, and then add this to the mixture in the pan.

3. Sift together the remaining sponge ingredients into a large bowl or into the bowl of a freestanding electric mixer. Using the mixer with the paddle attachment or a hand-held electric whisk, set on a low speed, pour in the contents of the pan.

Scrape down the sides of the bowl and continue to mix thoroughly until all the ingredients are incorporated.

4. Pour the batter into the prepared cake tin and bake for approximately 45 minutes or until the sponge bounces back when lightly pressed and a skewer inserted into the middle of the cake comes out clean. Set aside to cool, and then remove from the tin on to a wire rack, making sure the cake is cold to the touch before you frost it.

5. Using the electric whisk or the freestanding mixer with paddle attachment, mix the butter and icing sugar together until there are no large lumps of butter and it is fully combined with the sugar in a sandy mixture. Add the cream cheese and mix in a low speed, then increase the speed to medium and beat until the frosting is light and fluffy.

6. Place the cooled cake on to a plate or cake card and top generously with the cream cheese frosting. The cake can be decorated with a light dusting of cocoa powder.

Dean's recipe for *Townend Ruby Murray without the hurry*, aka Chicken Tikka Masala

Right you lovely people, get your filter tips 'round this old chestnut.

Serves 1 – 4

What ya gonna need:

Right, get yourself down to a respectable butcher or deli or Booths and get yourself at least 4 good quality skinned chicken breasts (experience dictates that purchased elsewhere, breasts might disintegrate in the pot!)

1 x thumb size portion of fresh ginger (okay, so some thumbs are bigger than others but the bigger the better!)

1 x medium size red chilli

A good handful of fresh coriander

2 x medium size onions

1 x 400g tin of chopped tomatoes

1 x 400g tin of coconut milk

½ 283g Patak's Tikka Masala Paste

1 x lemon, 200g carton of yoghurt and a handful of crushed almonds (for serving)

A good knob of butter

Sea-salt

Ground pepper

Rice (I'll come to that at the bottom)

To start off with…

On a chopping board (preferably bamboo, as less wear on your knives) de-seed and finely chop the chilli and ginger and add to a plate.

Pick the leaves from the coriander leaving the stalks. Finely chop the stalks and add to plate with ginger and chilli. The leaves will come in use later so please set aside.

Finely chop the onions.

Cut the chicken breasts into a reasonable size, 2cm length by 1-2cm wide (the chunkier – the better).

Down to business:

In a large frying pan (non-stick is better) or cooking pot add the knob of butter and heat until melted. In Townend we only use electric hobs so Mark 4 is pretty good, a medium to high heat, but the law of physics might dispute this.

Add the chopped onions and stir regularly until they start softening and brown.

Add the chopped ginger, chilli and coriander and keep stirring so the ingredients are well mixed.

Add the chicken and keep stirring until the chicken begins to brown.

Add half the jar of masala paste and stir thoroughly letting it blend in with the chicken until well coated.

Add chopped tomatoes and coconut milk and stir well.

Using one of the cans, add between a quarter to half a tin of fresh water (depending on the thickness) and turn the heat down to allow the mixture to simmer.

Add a reasonable dose of sea salt and pepper.

Allow to simmer for at least an hour or until excess water has boiled off so that the curry sauce is thick but not too runny. Add some of the coriander leaves to the simmer for that extra punch. Please stir regularly so that the meat and onions don't stick and burn on the bottom of pan.

The proof is in the eating…

Rice is not a speciality of mine so I tend to go with a two bags of boil in the bag basmati rice allowing 12 – 15 minutes in pot of salted boiling water. After all, the taste is in the curry itself.

Better still, if there's no rush, put the curry mix in a fridge overnight and let the chicken marinate – lovely jubbly!

However, if your punters are waiting and feeling peckish why not wack some naan bread in the oven, warm, then serve up with a good dollop of roughly chopped cucumber, fresh yoghurt and coriander – beautiful!

Time allowing I like to, using a small straight edge cup, fill with rice and turn upside down on plate to make a tower. Add the curry sauce and sprinkle with the remaining coriander leaves and crushed almonds (optional with yoghurt) and serve with a slice of lemon and a choice of wines. White is better.

Get it down ya!

Michael's recipe for Marbled Eggs

For Marbled Tea Eggs, you'll want to hard boil eggs first, and after they cool off, use a back of a teaspoon to gently crack the eggshell all over.
Keep the eggshell intact, but the more you crack, the more intricate the design of the marble will be.
Make those cracks pretty deep, as that is how the tea/soy mixture will seep into the egg.

Ingredients:

Egg
Black Tea
Soy sauce

Gently place the eggs in a medium pot and fill with water to cover the eggs by 1-inch.
Bring the pot to a boil, lower the heat and let simmer for 3 minutes.
Remove the eggs (leaving the water in the pot) and let cool under running cool water.
Using the back of the teaspoon, gently tap the eggshell to crack the shell all over.
The more you tap, the more intricate the design. Do this with a delicate hand to keep the shell intact.
To the same pot with the boiling water, return the eggs and add in the remaining ingredients.
Bring the mixture to a boil and immediately turn the heat to low.
Simmer for 40 minutes, cover with lid and let eggs steep for a few hours to overnight.
The longer you steep, the more flavourful and deeply marbled the tea eggs will be.

Andy's recipe for Alternative Gingerbread

4oz soft brown sugar

8oz self-raising flour

4oz butter

½ teaspoon bicarbonate soda

2 teaspoons ground ginger

1 tablespoon golden syrup

1oz candied Peel (cut fine if preferred)

2oz crystallized ginger (cut into small pieces)

Beat butter, sugar and syrup until soft and creamy. Stir in dry ingredients. Add candied peel and crystallized ginger. The mixture will be very dry but don't add any liquid. Spread ¼" thick in well-greased tray and cook in slow to moderate oven for 30 to 40 minutes. It should only be slightly brown.

Amanda's recipe for a simple dish of mushroom soup with a hunk of warm bread and butter.

So here goes:
1pt chicken stock
1pt fresh full fat milk
2oz butter
2oz plain flour
salt and lashings of cracked black pepper
fresh parsley
8oz button mushrooms (even if they are going a little black don't worry)

Method
(It's so easy even you, Mark, can't go wrong with this!)
Place stock, milk, butter and flour in a saucepan. Heat, stirring continuously until the mixture thickens and boils. Season, add parsley and mushrooms, cover and simmer gently for ten minutes. Remove from heat, add cream and parsley. Serve with warm bread and lashings of butter.

For pudding make: Black Magic

1/4pt fresh single cream
4oz plain flour
2 level teaspoons baking powder
2oz cocoa
5oz granulated sugar
1 teaspoon vanilla essence
3oz demerara sugar
12fl oz boiling water

Method
Pre heat oven 180 C, gas 4, 350 F.
Butter a 1.3ltr (2 ¼ pt) baking dish or soufflé dish.
Sieve flour with baking powder and 2 level tablespoons of cocoa into a bowl. Stir in the sugar vanilla essence and cream then beat until smooth. Spread the mixture into the buttered dish.
Mix the demerara sugar with the remaining cocoa powder and sprinkle it over the creamed mixture. Pour the boiling water all over the pudding then bake for about 50 minutes until risen and the sponge mixture (which will have come to the top) feels firm to the touch. Turn out if you get the chance or just spoon out, but remember to serve with Mrs Dowson's Ice cream. Enjoy. xx

Hung's recipe for Coffin Lid

Coffin Lid (Coffin Bread) is a very famous Taiwanese cuisine, which is also available in night markets. (Taiwan has numerous nice and fun night markets.) The pronunciation of "coffin" in Mandarin is similar with "getting promotion and becoming rich." So it's a symbol of good luck. [Even if it still sounds horrible to you, "bread bowl" is similar to "Coffin Lid".]

Ingredients:
1 whole loaf bread (uncut)
20g peas
20g chopped carrots
20g chopped potatoes
20g chopped onion
30g mushroom
Some seafood or diced chicken

Seasonings:
1 tablespoon salt
1 tablespoon butter
2 tablespoons plain flour
Some white pepper powder
Some milk

Directions:

1. Melt butter in a pan, cook onion until the fragrance is out and then add flour.
2. Add some milk and whisk gently until it mixes properly.
3. Put seafood/chicken, mushroom, peas, cooked carrot and potatoes in. When everything is cooked, leave it to one side.
4. Cut the bread into 3-4cm thick slices and deep fry in the oil until golden and crispy.
5. Cut a square into the bread, to make a lid – but be careful not to cut all the way through (make it like a square bowl).
6. Fill the bread with the stew (step 1-3) and put the lid back on.
7. Enjoy!

Colin's Leftover Chicken Pasties

First make a Béchamel sauce:

Melt 15g butter in a saucepan and stir in 15g flour.

Cook for approximately 1 minute, until the mixture colours slightly.

Remove the saucepan from the heat and gradually add 300ml of milk, whisking constantly.

Season with salt and pepper and add a chopped raw leek.

Return saucepan to the heat and cook, stirring regularly, until the sauce is thick and smooth. Simmer gently for a couple of minutes.

Take off the heat, stir in your cooked leftover chicken and leave to cool.

Next, roll your pastry into circles, put the desired amount of filling down the middle, brush egg-wash around the circumference, bring the edges of your circle to the top and crimp.

Put the pasties on a baking tray and into a preheated oven (180, gas mark 4) for about 20 – 25 minutes, until the pastry is cooked.

Mrs Mitchell's Dorset Apple Cake

Recipe from Mum. I am not a great cook!

8 oz self-raising flour
1/2 level teaspoonful cinnamon
4 oz butter
4 oz soft brown sugar
2 eggs
2 oz raisins or sultanas
2 cooking apples, stewed and pulped

Method

Heat oven to 325 f / Gas mark 3
Mix together all ingredients
Turn mixture into a greased loaf tin and bake just below centre of oven for about 1 1/2 hours.
Turn out and cool or leave in tin to cool.
Can be served in slices and buttered.

A really gorgeous recipe.